Editor
Erica N. Russikoff, M.A.

Contributing Editor
Karen McRae

Illustrators
Mark Mason
Renée Christine Yates

Cover Artist
Tony Carrillo

Editor in Chief
Ina Massler Levin, M.A.

Creative Director
Karen J. Goldfluss, M.S. Ed.

Imaging
Rosa C. See

Publisher

Mary D. Smith, M.S. Ed.

Teacher Created Resources
12621 Western Avenue
Garden Grove, CA 92841
www.teachercreated.com

ISBN: 978-1-4206-8842-9

©2010 Teacher Created Resources, Inc.
Reprinted, 2020 (PO602782)

Made in U.S.A.

Table of Contents

Monday	Math: *Tens and Ones*
	Reading: *Picture the Consonants*
Tuesday	Math: *Two Different Ways*
	Writing: *Edit and Write*
Wednesday	Math: *More or Less?*
	Reading: *What Will Happen?*
Thursday	Math: *Counting Chart*
	Writing: *Action Sentences*
Friday	Friday Fun: *Gumball Numbers, Alphabet Soup*

Monday	Math: *Number Line*
	Writing: *Which Mark?*
Tuesday	Math: *What's Missing?*
	Reading: *Rhyming Words*
Wednesday	Math: *Addition Practice*
	Writing: *Writing Details*
Thursday	Math: *Secret Number*
	Reading: *Look for Clues*
Friday	Friday Fun: *Magic Maze, Farm Fun*

Monday	Math: *Take Some Away*
	Reading: *Where in the Word?*
Tuesday	Math: *Odd or Even?*
	Writing: *Person, Place, or Thing?*
Wednesday	Math: *Flower Power*
	Reading: *Grandma's Mix-Up*
Thursday	Math: *Cool Scoops*
	Writing: *Stretch It Out*
Friday	Friday Fun: *Dive In, Scrambled Words*

Monday	Math: *Weight*
	Writing: *Contraction Match*
Tuesday	Math: *Length*
	Reading: *Can You Hear It?*
Wednesday	Math: *Which Holds More?*
	Writing: *Adding Adjectives*
Thursday	Math: *Tick-Tock*
	Reading: *Best Friends*
Friday	Friday Fun: *Fly Away, Ants on Parade*

Monday	Math: *Pieces and Wholes*
	Reading: *Combine Them*
Tuesday	Math: *Matching Shapes*
	Writing: *Spelling Practice*

Table of Contents *(cont.)*

A Message From the
National Summer Learning Association

Dear Parents,

Did you know that all young people experience learning losses when they don't engage in educational activities during the summer? That means some of what they've spent time learning over the preceding school year evaporates during the summer months. However, summer learning loss *is* something that you can help prevent. Summer is the perfect time for fun and engaging activities that can help children maintain and grow their academic skills. Here are just a few:

- ☼ Read with your child every day. Visit your local library together, and select books on subjects that interest your child.

- ☼ Ask your child's teacher for recommendations of books for summer reading. The Summer Reading List in this publication is a good start.

- ☼ Explore parks, nature preserves, museums, and cultural centers.

- ☼ Consider every day as a day full of teachable moments. Measuring in recipes and reviewing maps before a car trip are ways to learn or reinforce a skill. Use the Learning Experiences in the back of this book for more ideas.

- ☼ Each day, set goals to accomplish. For example, do five math problems or read a chapter in a book.

- ☼ Encourage your child to complete the activities in books, such as *Summertime Learning*, to help bridge the summer learning gap.

Our vision is for every child to be safe, healthy, and engaged in learning during the summer. Learn more at *www.summerlearning.org* and *www.summerlearningcampaign.org*.

Have a *memorable* summer!

Ron Fairchild
Chief Executive Officer
National Summer Learning Association

How to Use This Book

As a parent, you know that summertime is a time for fun and learning. So it is quite useful that fun and learning can go hand in hand when your child uses *Summertime Learning*.

There are many ways to use this book effectively with your child. We list three ideas on page 6. (See "Day by Day," "Pick and Choose," and "All of a Kind.") You may choose one way on one day, and, on another day, choose something else.

Book Organization

Summertime Learning is organized around an eight-week summer vacation period. For each weekday, there are two lessons. Each Monday through Thursday, there is a math lesson. Additionally, during the odd-numbered weeks, there is a reading lesson on Monday and Wednesday and a writing lesson on Tuesday and Thursday. During the even-numbered weeks, these lessons switch days. (Reading lessons are on Tuesday and Thursday, and writing lessons are on Monday and Wednesday.) Friday features two Friday Fun activities (one typically being a puzzle). The calendar looks like this:

Day	Week 1	Week 2	Week 3	Week 4	Week 5	Week 6	Week 7	Week 8
M	Math Reading	Math Writing	Math Reading	Math Writing	Math Reading	Math Writing	Math Reading	Math Writing
T	Math Writing	Math Reading	Math Writing	Math Reading	Math Writing	Math Reading	Math Writing	Math Reading
W	Math Reading	Math Writing	Math Reading	Math Writing	Math Reading	Math Writing	Math Reading	Math Writing
Th	Math Writing	Math Reading	Math Writing	Math Reading	Math Writing	Math Reading	Math Writing	Math Reading
F	Friday Fun Friday Fun	Friday Fun Friday Fun	Friday Fun Friday Fun	Friday Fun Friday Fun	Friday Fun Friday Fun	Friday Fun Friday Fun	Friday Fun Friday Fun	Friday Fun Friday Fun

How to Use This Book
(cont.)

Day by Day

You can have your child do the activities in order, beginning on the first Monday of summer vacation. He or she can complete the two lessons provided for each day. It does not matter if math, reading, or writing is completed first. The pages are designed so that each day of the week's lessons are back to back. The book is also perforated. This gives you the option of tearing the pages out for your child to work on. If you opt to have your child tear out the pages, you might want to store the completed pages in a special folder or three-ring binder that your child decorates.

Pick and Choose

You may find that you do not want to have your child work strictly in order. Feel free to pick and choose any combination of pages based on your child's needs and interests.

All of a Kind

Perhaps your child needs more help in one area than another. You may opt to have him or her work only on math, reading, or writing.

Keeping Track

A Reward Chart is included on page 10 of this book, so you and your child can keep track of the activities that have been completed. This page is designed to be used with the stickers provided. Once your child has finished a page, have him or her put a sticker on the castle. If you don't want to use stickers for this, have your child color in a circle each time an activity is completed.

The stickers can also be used on the individual pages. As your child finishes a page, let him or her place a sticker in the sun at the top of the page. If he or she asks where to begin the next day, simply have him or her start on the page after the last sticker.

There are enough stickers to use for both the Reward Chart and the sun on each page. Plus, there are extra stickers for your child to enjoy.

Standards and Skills

Each activity in *Summertime Learning* meets one or more of the following standards and skills*. Visit *http://www.teachercreated.com/standards/* for correlations to the Common Core State Standards. The activities in this book are designed to help your child reinforce the skills learned during first grade, as well as introduce new skills that will be learned in second grade.

Language Arts Standards

- Uses the general skills and strategies of the writing process
- Uses grammatical and mechanical conventions in written compositions
- Uses the general skills and strategies of the reading process
- Uses reading skills and strategies to understand and interpret a variety of literary texts
- Uses reading skills and strategies to understand and interpret a variety of informational texts

Mathematics Standards

- Uses a variety of strategies in the problem-solving process
- Understands and applies basic and advanced properties of the concepts of numbers
- Uses basic and advanced procedures while performing the processes of computation
- Understands and applies basic and advanced properties of the concepts of measurement
- Understands and applies basic and advanced properties of the concepts of geometry
- Understands and applies basic and advanced concepts of statistics and data analysis

Writing Skills

- Evaluates own and others' writing
- Uses strategies to organize written work
- Uses writing and other methods to describe familiar persons, places, objects, or experiences
- Writes in a variety of forms or genres
- Writes for different purposes
- Uses conventions of print in writing
- Uses complete sentences in written compositions
- Uses nouns in written compositions
- Uses verbs in written compositions
- Uses adjectives in written compositions
- Uses adverbs in written compositions
- Uses conventions of spelling in written compositions

Standards and Skills

(cont.)

Writing Skills *(cont.)*

- ✿ Uses conventions of capitalization in written compositions
- ✿ Uses conventions of punctuation in written compositions

Reading Skills

- ✿ Uses basic elements of phonetic analysis to decode unknown words
- ✿ Uses basic elements of structural analysis to decode unknown words
- ✿ Understands level-appropriate sight words and vocabulary
- ✿ Knows setting, main characters, main events, sequence, and problems in stories
- ✿ Knows the main ideas or theme of a story
- ✿ Relates stories to personal experiences
- ✿ Uses reading skills and strategies to understand a variety of informational texts
- ✿ Understands the main idea and supporting details of simple expository information
- ✿ Summarizes information found in texts
- ✿ Relates new information to prior knowledge and experience

Mathematics Skills

- ✿ Draws pictures to represent problems
- ✿ Explains to others how she or he went about solving a numerical problem
- ✿ Makes organized lists or tables of information necessary for solving a problem
- ✿ Uses whole number models to represent problems
- ✿ Understands symbolic, concrete, and pictorial representations of numbers
- ✿ Understands basic whole-number relationships
- ✿ Understands the concept of a unit and its subdivision into equal parts
- ✿ Adds and subtracts whole numbers
- ✿ Solves real-world problems involving addition and subtraction of whole numbers
- ✿ Understands basic estimation strategies and terms
- ✿ Understands the inverse relationship between addition and subtraction
- ✿ Understands the basic measures length, width, height, weight, and temperature
- ✿ Understands the concept of time and how it is measured
- ✿ Knows processes for telling time, counting money, and measuring length, weight, and temperature, using basic standard and nonstandard units

Mathematics Skills *(cont.)*

✿ Understands basic properties of and similarities and differences between simple geometric shapes

✿ Understands the common language of spatial sense

✿ Collects and represents information about objects or events in simple graphs

* Standards and skills used with permission from McREL (Copyright 2009, McREL. Midcontinent Research for Education and Learning. Address: 4601 DTC Boulevard, Suite 500, Denver, CO 80237. Telephone: 303-337-0990. Web site: www.mcrel.org/standards-benchmarks)

Reward Chart

10 ©Teacher Created Resources, Inc.

Tens and Ones

Directions: Each box of crayons holds 10 crayons or one set of ten. Each single crayon is one. Count each set of tens and ones. Write the number of tens and ones. Then, write the total number on the line. The first one has been done for you.

1.

_____1_____ tens _____6_____ one(s)

_____16_____

2.

_____ tens _____ one(s)

_____

3.

_____ tens _____ one(s)

_____

4.

_____ tens _____ one(s)

_____

5.

_____ tens _____ one(s)

_____

6.

_____ tens _____ one(s)

_____

Picture the Consonants

Directions: Say the name of each picture below. Print the letter for its beginning sound and its ending sound. Then, trace the whole word.

1. a	2. u	3. u	4. a
5. oo	6. e	7. e	8. i
9. a	10. ee	11. u	12. u

Two Different Ways

Directions: Show two different coin combinations that equal the amount shown. Draw simple coin pictures or use numbers and words. The first one has been done for you.

	Way #1	Way #2
1. 5¢	1 nickel	5 pennies
2. 11¢		
3. 25¢		
4. 50¢		
5. 6¢		
6. 15¢		

Edit and Write

Directions: Rewrite the sentences below using correct capitalization and punctuation. The first one has been done for you.

1. may i go to the beach on friday

   <u>May I go to the beach on Friday?</u>

2. the beach is a fun place to go in july

   _____

3. did you see that bird fly over jessica's head

   _____

4. my friend julian and i like to ride the waves

   _____

5. look out for that foaming, white wave

   _____

6. what can you find at the beach in august

   _____

7. at the beach, i saw sand seaweed and rocks

   _____

8. on sunday, a big, orange crab crawled across my towel

   _____

More or Less?

Math

Directions: Use the < (less than), > (greater than), or = (equal to) symbols below to compare the numbers. Then, complete each sentence.

1.

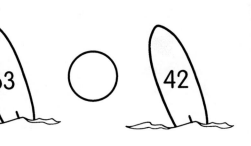

_____ is greater than _____.

2.

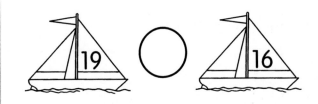

_____ is greater than _____.

3.

_____ is less than _____.

4.

_____ is greater than _____.

5.

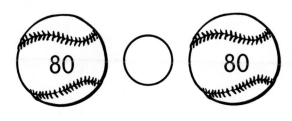

_____ is equal to _____.

6.

_____ is less than _____.

©Teacher Created Resources, Inc.

#8842 Summertime Learning

What Will Happen?

Directions: A good reader likes to predict what is going to happen next. Read the sentences below. Predict what will happen next. Then, write your answer on the lines.

1. Kevin poured himself a glass of juice. Then, he spilled the juice on the floor.

   _____

   _____

2. Maya heard the phone ring, so she went to answer it.

   _____

   _____

3. The man on the radio said there was snow on the way. The temperature was below freezing, and the sky was filled with clouds.

   _____

   _____

4. Sandra had a spelling test on Friday. On Thursday, she practiced all the words and could spell each one.

   _____

   _____

Counting Chart

Math

Directions: Complete the chart by adding the missing numbers. Then, follow the instructions below.

61	62			65	66		
69		71					76
	79			82	83		
	86			89	90		92
	94	95		97		99	

1. Color the numbers with a **0** in the ones place red.

2. Draw a yellow circle around the numbers with a **6** in the tens place.

3. Draw a green square around the numbers with the same digit in the tens and the ones places.

4. Draw a blue star on the numbers with a **3** in the ones place.

5. Draw a purple line under the numbers that have a **7** in the tens or ones places.

Action Sentences

Directions: Write a verb for each picture. Then, write a sentence using the verb. The first one has been done for you.

	Verb	Sentence
1.	eat	The girl eats a peach.
2.		
3.		
4.		
5.		

18

©Teacher Created Resources, Inc.

Gumball Numbers

Directions: Color the gumballs using the Color Key.

Color Key

1 — 20 **Red**   61 — 80 **Green**

21 — 40 **Orange**   81 — 100 **Yellow**

41 — 60 **Blue**

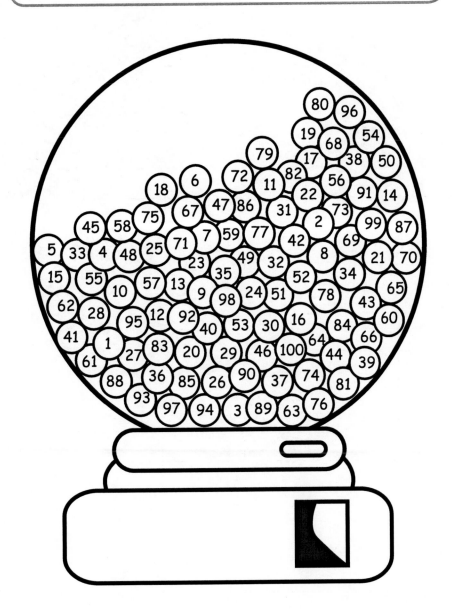

Alphabet Soup

Directions: Search for words in the bowl of soup below. Circle or color each word as you find it. Can you find them all? One word is not in the bowl of soup.

DOWN	KNOW	THAT	THEY	YOU
FROM	MADE	THEIR	WITH	YOUR

Which word is missing? _____

Number Line

Directions: Use the number line to help you solve the following problems.

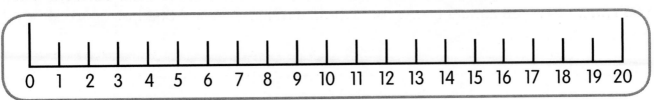

1. Start on 5. Count forward 7.
   What number are you on?

   _____

2. Start on 4. Count forward 10.
   What number are you on?

   _____

3. Start on 8. Count forward 10.
   What number are you on?

   _____

4. Start on 6. Count forward 9.
   What number are you on?

   _____

5. Start on 9. Count forward 9.
   What number are you on?

   _____

6. Start on 7. Count forward 0.
   What number are you on?

   _____

Directions: Continue to use the number line to help you solve the addition problems.

7.
$$\begin{array}{r} 3 \\ + 9 \\ \hline \end{array}$$

8.
$$\begin{array}{r} 5 \\ + 8 \\ \hline \end{array}$$

9.
$$\begin{array}{r} 13 \\ + 3 \\ \hline \end{array}$$

10.
$$\begin{array}{r} 0 \\ + 11 \\ \hline \end{array}$$

Which Mark?

Directions: Read each sentence below. Decide if the sentence is a statement or a question. Circle the correct ending punctuation mark. The first one has been done for you.

1. When is your birthday	• (?)
2. My birthday is in June	• ?
3. I am going to have a party	• ?
4. Will you be able to come	• ?
5. We can play games	• ?
6. My mom will bake a cake	• ?
7. What is your favorite flavor	• ?
8. I hope my friends bring presents	• ?

22

©Teacher Created Resources, Inc.

What's Missing?

An **addend** is a number that is added to another to form a sum.

Directions: Find the missing addends. Then, use the letters to answer the question below.

1. $3 +$ _____ $= 4$ **E**	6. _____ $+ 0 = 10$ **D**
2. $3 +$ _____ $= 8$ **H**	7. _____ $+ 2 = 9$ **I**
3. _____ $+ 5 = 9$ **R**	8. $8 +$ _____ $= 8$ **S**
4. $4 +$ _____ $= 7$ **O**	9. $1 +$ _____ $= 9$ **L**
5. _____ $+ 5 = 7$ **T**	10. $3 +$ _____ $= 9$ **G**

Why did the chicken cross the playground?

__ __   __ __ __   __ __   __ __ __

2   3   6   1   2   2   3   2   5   1

__ __ __ __ __   __ __ __ __ __.

3   2   5   1   4   0   8   7   10   1

    23

Rhyming Words

Directions: Complete the rhyming words below. The first one has been done for you.

1. **cat**

   rat   bat

6. **meat**

   h___   s___

2. **tent**

   w___   d___

7. **cake**

   b___   w___

3. **sun**

   b___   f___

8. **pig**

   w___   f___

4. **bike**

   l___   h___

9. **rose**

   n___   h___

5. **goat**

   b___   c___

10. **dog**

    f___   l___

Addition Practice

Math

Directions: Complete the problems below.

1.
$$\begin{array}{r} 5 \\ +\ 11 \\ \hline \end{array}$$

2.
$$\begin{array}{r} 14 \\ +\ 0 \\ \hline \end{array}$$

3.
$$\begin{array}{r} 13 \\ +\ 1 \\ \hline \end{array}$$

4.
$$\begin{array}{r} 11 \\ +\ 4 \\ \hline \end{array}$$

5.
$$\begin{array}{r} 12 \\ +\ 5 \\ \hline \end{array}$$

6.
$$\begin{array}{r} 10 \\ +\ 2 \\ \hline \end{array}$$

7.
$$\begin{array}{r} 3 \\ +\ 12 \\ \hline \end{array}$$

8.
$$\begin{array}{r} 7 \\ +\ 10 \\ \hline \end{array}$$

9.
$$\begin{array}{r} 5 \\ +\ 13 \\ \hline \end{array}$$

10.
$$\begin{array}{r} 8 \\ +\ 6 \\ \hline \end{array}$$

11.
$$\begin{array}{r} 7 \\ +\ 9 \\ \hline \end{array}$$

12.
$$\begin{array}{r} 6 \\ +\ 9 \\ \hline \end{array}$$

13.
$$\begin{array}{r} 15 \\ +\ 3 \\ \hline \end{array}$$

14.
$$\begin{array}{r} 14 \\ +\ 3 \\ \hline \end{array}$$

15.
$$\begin{array}{r} 2 \\ +\ 11 \\ \hline \end{array}$$

Mental Math

Directions: Can you add the numbers in your head? Write your answers on the lines.

16. $1 + 1 + 1 =$ _____

17. $5 + 1 + 4 =$ _____

18. $1 + 2 + 3 =$ _____

19. $2 + 4 + 6 =$ _____

Writing Details

Directions: Choose two or more detail sentences to support each main idea. Write your answers on the lines.

My sister is funny.

_____

_____

_____

Details

☼ She wears strange clothes.
☼ She never does her homework.
☼ She is nice to my brother.
☼ She loves pizza.
☼ My sister even dyed her hair blue.

I love to watch my mom cook.

_____

_____

_____

Details

☼ When she cooks bacon, the fat splatters all over the stove. Gross!
☼ Everything she makes smells so good.
☼ Sometimes she lets me lick the bowl.
☼ She gives me little bites of my favorite foods.
☼ I am learning to be a bad cook by watching her.

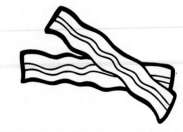

Secret Number

Directions: To discover the secret number, find the sums and follow the instructions below.

1.
$$\begin{array}{r} 21 \\ + 18 \\ \hline \end{array}$$

2.
$$\begin{array}{r} 31 \\ + 16 \\ \hline \end{array}$$

3.
$$\begin{array}{r} 31 \\ + 21 \\ \hline \end{array}$$

4.
$$\begin{array}{r} 41 \\ + 31 \\ \hline \end{array}$$

5.
$$\begin{array}{r} 12 \\ + 12 \\ \hline \end{array}$$

6.
$$\begin{array}{r} 10 \\ + 17 \\ \hline \end{array}$$

☼ It is not the number **24**. Cross it out.

☼ It is not the number **39**. Cross it out.

☼ It is not the number **52**. Cross it out.

☼ It is not the number **72**. Cross it out.

☼ It is not the number **47**. Cross it out.

What is the secret number? _____

Look for Clues

Directions: Detectives look for clues. You can also look for clues as long as you pay close attention! Look at the pictures below. Use clues from the pictures to answer the questions.

1. Is this boy enjoying himself? How can you tell?

_____

_____

2. Are these three children friends? How can you tell?

_____

_____

3. How do these two children know each other? How can you tell?

_____

_____

4. How does this girl feel? How can you tell?

_____

_____

Magic Maze

Directions: Help the wizard find his wand. Start at the wizard, and color the path of equations that equal **19**.

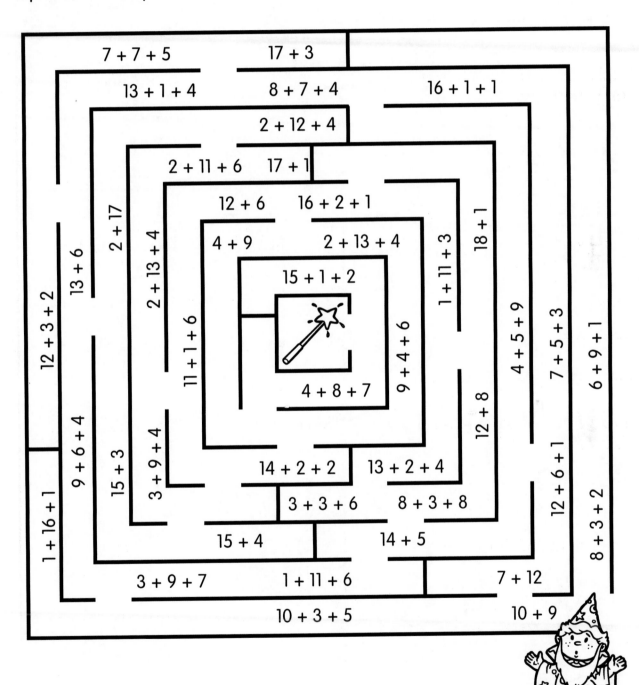

Farm Fun

Directions: How many long-vowel words can you find in the picture? Circle all of them. Then, color the picture.

Take Some Away

Directions: Read each problem below. Follow the instructions. The first one has been done for you.

1. Count the mice. Cross out 3 mice. Write the numerals on the lines to show the subtraction problem and answer.

___6___ – ___3___ = ___3___

2. Count the ladybugs. Cross out 5 ladybugs. Write the numerals on the lines to show the subtraction problem and answer.

_____ – _____ = _____

3. Count the penguins. Cross out 2 penguins. Write the numerals on the lines to show the subtraction problem and answer.

_____ – _____ = _____

4. Count the bees. Cross out 4 bees. Write the numerals on the lines to show the subtraction problem and answer.

_____ – _____ = _____

5. Count the monkeys. Cross out 0 monkeys. Write the numerals on the lines to show the subtraction problem and answer.

_____ – _____ = _____

Where in the Word?

Directions: Use every word in the Word Bank to complete the chart below. Find the words that have that specific letter as the beginning, middle, and final consonant. Write each word in the correct column. The first one has been done for you.

Word Bank

apple	duck	gift	leaf	nut	sack
camel	eggs	gum	lid	play	tent
cup	fall	ladder	milk	rain	vest

	Beginning Consonant	Middle Consonant	Final Consonant
d	duck	ladder	lid
f			
m			
n			
p			
s			

Odd or Even?

Math

Directions: Solve the subtraction problems below. Then, color the boxes using the key.

> ### Key
>
> Odd = **Blue**   Even = **Red**

1. $\begin{array}{r} 9 \\ -\ 4 \\ \hline \end{array}$	2. $\begin{array}{r} 6 \\ -\ 5 \\ \hline \end{array}$	3. $\begin{array}{r} 7 \\ -\ 2 \\ \hline \end{array}$	4. $\begin{array}{r} 8 \\ -\ 3 \\ \hline \end{array}$
5. $\begin{array}{r} 5 \\ -\ 2 \\ \hline \end{array}$	6. $\begin{array}{r} 8 \\ -\ 6 \\ \hline \end{array}$	7. $\begin{array}{r} 9 \\ -\ 5 \\ \hline \end{array}$	8. $\begin{array}{r} 6 \\ -\ 3 \\ \hline \end{array}$
9. $\begin{array}{r} 1 \\ -\ 0 \\ \hline \end{array}$	10. $\begin{array}{r} 5 \\ -\ 3 \\ \hline \end{array}$	11. $\begin{array}{r} 6 \\ -\ 4 \\ \hline \end{array}$	12. $\begin{array}{r} 4 \\ -\ 1 \\ \hline \end{array}$
13. $\begin{array}{r} 9 \\ -\ 6 \\ \hline \end{array}$	14. $\begin{array}{r} 8 \\ -\ 5 \\ \hline \end{array}$	15. $\begin{array}{r} 7 \\ -\ 4 \\ \hline \end{array}$	16. $\begin{array}{r} 3 \\ -\ 2 \\ \hline \end{array}$

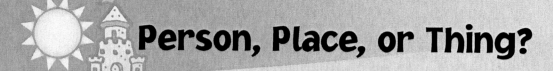

Person, Place, or Thing?

Directions: Read each sentence below. Identify the nouns in the sentence. Write the nouns on the correct lines. The first one has been done for you.

1. Dad rode a bike to the park.

Dad	park	bike
person	place	thing

2. The performers sang a song at the theater.

person	place	thing

3. The pool was full of children in bathing suits.

person	place	thing

4. The queen wore her crown in the castle.

person	place	thing

5. The boy returned the book to the library.

person	place	thing

Flower Power

Directions: Solve all of the subtraction problems. Then, color the correct petals that match the number in the center of the flower.

1.

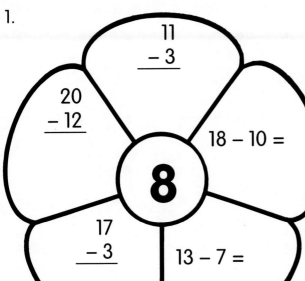

$$11 - 3$$

$$20 - 12$$

$$18 - 10 =$$

8

$$17 - 3$$

$$13 - 7 =$$

2.

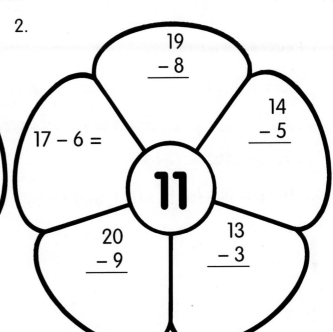

$$19 - 8$$

$$14 - 5$$

$$17 - 6 =$$

11

$$20 - 9$$

$$13 - 3$$

3.

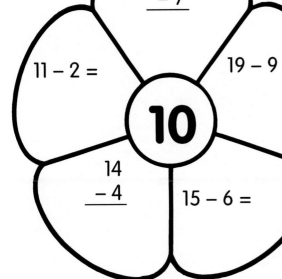

$$17 - 7$$

$$11 - 2 =$$

$$19 - 9 =$$

10

$$14 - 4$$

$$15 - 6 =$$

4.

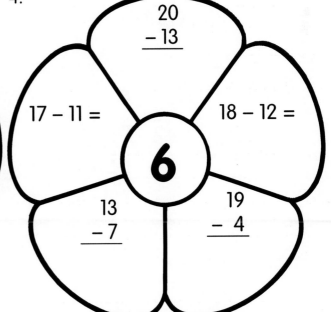

$$20 - 13$$

$$17 - 11 =$$

$$18 - 12 =$$

6

$$13 - 7$$

$$19 - 4$$

Grandma's Mix-Up

Directions: This story is all mixed up. See if you can rewrite the story in the order that it should go.

I picked out a bird.

We definitely had a wonderful day at the pet store!

Today, my grandma took me to the pet store.

I named it Bailey.

After she paid for the bird, I could not wait to get Bailey home.

At the pet store, Grandma said I could get a pet.

_____

_____

_____

_____

_____

_____

_____

Cool Scoops

Directions: Fill in the missing number on each cone to complete the problem.

1.

10
+
16

2.

17
– 8

3.

+ 4
17

4.

9
+
19

5.

8
–
1

6.

15
+ 4

7.

– 11
7

8.

21
–16

9.

20
+
29

10.

14
– 7

11.

–13
10

12.

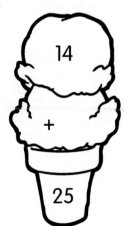

14
+
25

Stretch It Out

Directions: Practice writing longer sentences by rewriting each sentence. Add at least two more words to make the sentence more interesting.

Example: The dog barked.

The little, brown dog barked daily.

1. She loves to read.

_____

_____

2. Laura had a bike.

_____

_____

3. He is my friend.

_____

_____

4. Do you like cake?

_____

_____

Dive In

Directions: Solve the problems. Use a blue crayon to color the areas with a difference of more than 10. Use a gray crayon to color the areas with a difference of less than 10.

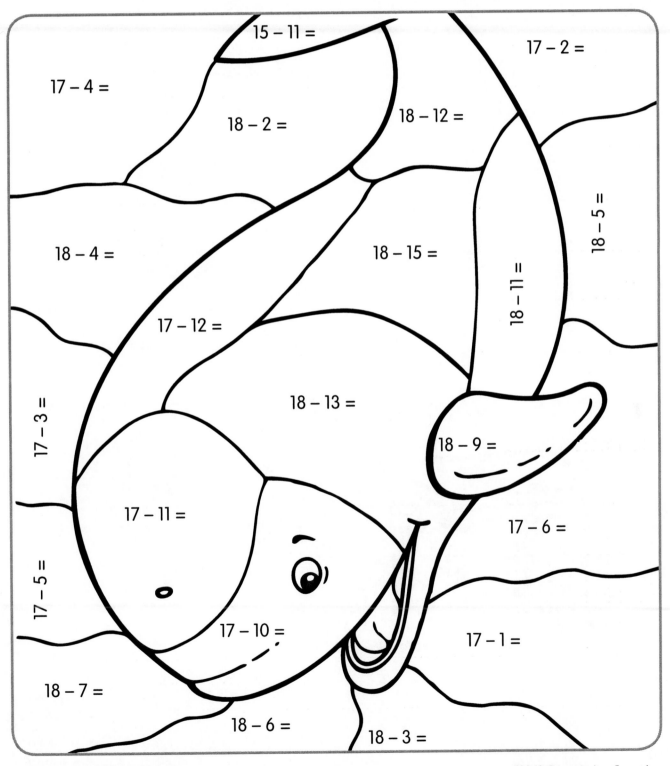

15 – 11 =

17 – 2 =

17 – 4 =

18 – 2 =

18 – 12 =

18 – 5 =

18 – 4 =

18 – 15 =

18 – 11 =

17 – 12 =

17 – 3 =

18 – 13 =

18 – 9 =

17 – 11 =

17 – 6 =

17 – 5 =

17 – 10 =

17 – 1 =

18 – 7 =

18 – 6 =

18 – 3 =

Scrambled Words

Directions: Unscramble the letters to find the things used in a house.

1. dbe _____

2. mlpa _____

3. voen _____

4. lvsnteeiio _____

5. batle _____

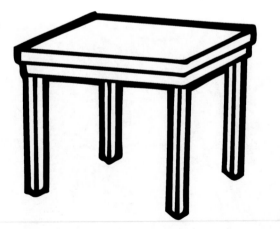

6. nkis _____

7. sagsl _____

8. hraic _____

9. lewto _____

10. ponso _____

Weight

Math

Directions: Number the pictures 1, 2, or 3, going from lightest (1) to heaviest (3). The first one has been done for you.

1.

   3   I   2

2.

_____   _____   _____

3.

_____   _____   _____

4.

_____   _____   _____

Directions: Which weighs more? Use the **>** (greater than) or **<** (less than) symbol. The first one has been done for you.

5.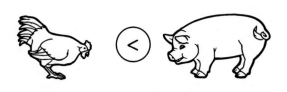

6.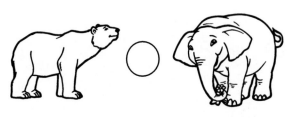

7.

8.

©Teacher Created Resources, Inc.

#8842 Summertime Learning

Contraction Match

A **contraction** is a short form of a word or words. For example, "don't" is a contraction for *do* and *not*. When you form a contraction, you use an apostrophe to connect the words.

Directions: Place an apostrophe in the contractions below. Then, draw a line connecting the contraction to the words that are used to form it. The first one has been done for you.

Contractions	Words
1. they're	I have
2. didnt	she is
3. Ive	here is
4. Im	you are
5. youre	did not
6. wouldnt	we are
7. lets	let us
8. shes	I am
9. were	would not
10. heres	they are

Length

Math

Directions: Each section of the bar equals one inch. Measure each item to the nearest inch. The first one has been done for you.

1.

The bat is __2__ inches long.

2.

The baseball glove is _____ inch long.

3.

The ice skates are _____ inches long.

4.

The volleyball is _____ inch long.

5.

The soccer balls are _____ inches long.

6.

The bowling pins are _____ inches long.

Can You Hear It?

> A **consonant digraph** is two consonants that make one sound. You can hear consonant digraphs in *shop, chip, that, where,* and *pick.*

Directions: Read each sentence. Circle the word that has the consonant digraph *sh, ch, th, wh,* or *ck.* Then, think of another word that uses the same consonant digraph, and write it on the line. The first one has been done for you.

1. I have two (thumbs).   *think*

2. Most shells are pretty.   _____

3. A cherry is a small fruit.   _____

4. A person can think.   _____

5. Shoes go on feet.   _____

6. A duck is yellow.   _____

7. I can sit on a chair.   _____

8. You can blow a whistle.   _____

9. A candle has a wick.   _____

10. A shuttle can fly in space.   _____

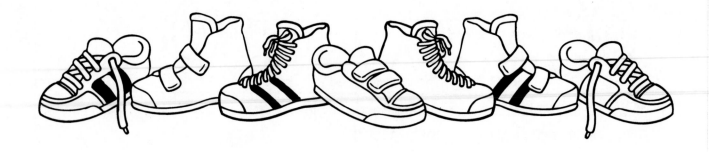

Which Holds More?

Directions: Color the containers that would hold more.

1.

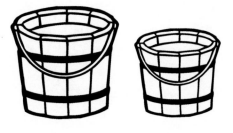

2.

3.

4.

5.

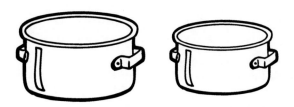

6.

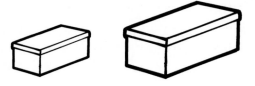

7.

8.

Adding Adjectives

> **Adjectives** are words that describe nouns. They help a reader "see" what the noun is like.

Directions: Add adjectives to the sentences below. Use the Word Bank to help you.

Word Bank

beautiful	blue	furry	red
big	crisp	little	shiny
black	fast	loud	shy

1. The _____ , _____ fire engine roared down the street.

2. The _____ , _____ girl was scared.

3. The _____ , _____ cats meowed softly.

4. The _____ , _____ apple tasted good.

5. The _____ , _____ bug walked across the floor.

6. The _____ , _____ bird sat on the wire.

46

©Teacher Created Resources, Inc.

Tick-Tock

Directions: Draw the hands to show half an hour later. Write the time on the line. The first one has been done for you.

1.

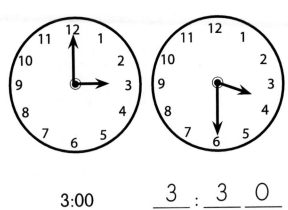

3:00   __3__ : __3__ __0__

2.

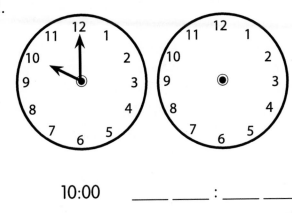

10:00   ____ ____ : ____ ____

Directions: Read the problem. Draw the hands on the clock to show the ending time. Then, write the time on the line.

3. The piano lesson began at 2:00 and lasted half an hour. What time did the lesson end?

____ : ____ ____

4. Band practice began at 4:00 and lasted half an hour. What time did the practice end?

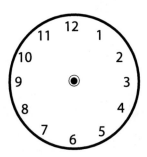

____ : ____ ____

5. The violin lesson began at 1:00 and lasted half an hour. What time did the lesson end?

____ : ____ ____

6. The singing lesson began at 12:00 and lasted half an hour. What time did the lesson end?

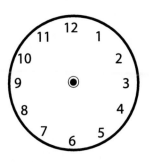

____ ____ : ____ ____

Best Friends

Directions: Read the story, and then answer the questions.

Martha and Janis are best friends. Every afternoon, the girls do their homework together. They munch on their favorite snack, popcorn. After they finish their homework, Martha and Janis go to the park. Martha takes her skates. She is a great skater. Janis brings her scooter. When Pete comes along, all the children go on the swings and the slides. They all enjoy that. It is good to have a best friend.

1.   Who are the best friends?_____

2.   What do the girls do in the afternoon? _____

_____

3.   Where do the girls go when they are done with their homework?

_____

4.   What do the girls do at the park?_____

_____

_____

5.   Who is your best friend? _____

Fly Away

Directions: Draw the other half of the object below, using the squares as a guide. Then, color the picture.

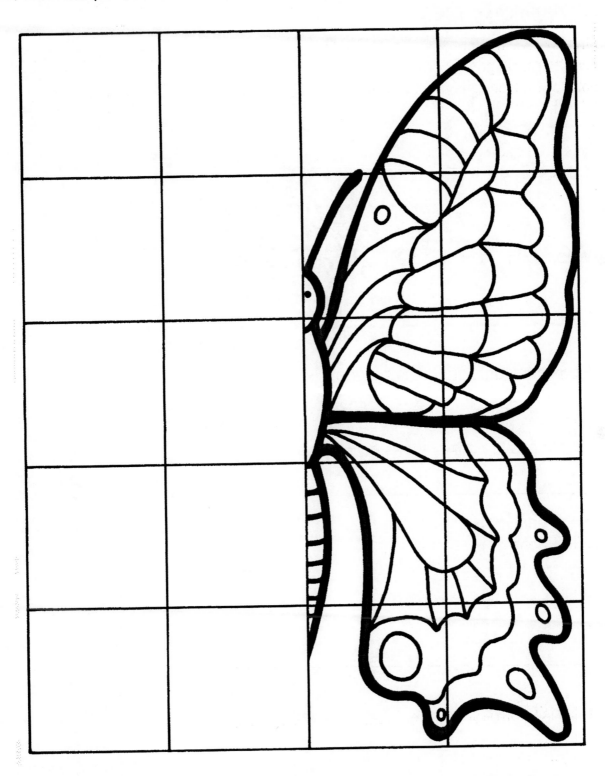

Ants on Parade

Directions: Take a long look at the picture. Try to remember everything you see. Then, cover the picture, and answer as many questions as you can without looking back at the picture.

1. How many ants are in the parade?

   _____

2. What does the ant in shorts have on its head?

   _____

3. How many ants are holding the slice of watermelon?

   _____

4. Who is leading the parade?

   _____

5. What did the last ant almost drop?

   _____

Pieces and Wholes

Directions: Shade the appropriate sections of the circles. Then, solve the problem.

1. Tucker made 2 pies. Tucker ate $\frac{1}{6}$ of one pie. His brother, Taylor, ate $\frac{1}{4}$ of the other pie. Who ate more pie?

   _____ ate more pie.

   $\frac{1}{6}$ $\frac{1}{4}$

2. Lindsey ate $\frac{2}{3}$ of a pizza. Phil ate $\frac{2}{4}$ of a pizza. Who ate more pizza?

   _____ ate more pizza.

   $\frac{2}{3}$ $\frac{2}{4}$

3. Sharon caught 4 out of 5 fly balls. Chad caught 4 out of 9 fly balls. Who did the best overall?

   _____ did the best overall.

   $\frac{4}{5}$ $\frac{4}{9}$

4. Mary spelled 6 of the 7 words correctly. Seth spelled 1 of the 6 words correctly. Which one earned the higher spelling score?

   _____ earned the higher score.

   $\frac{6}{7}$ $\frac{1}{6}$

5. In basketball, Cori made 1 basket out of 8 tries. Danny made 2 baskets out of 4 tries. Who had the higher shooting score?

   _____ had the higher shooting score.

   $\frac{1}{8}$ $\frac{2}{4}$

Combine Them

Directions: Look at each picture. Write the words that name the pictures on the short lines. Then, write the words together to make a compound word. Use the Word Bank to help you.

Word Bank

ball	dog	house	sea
bow	foot	rain	shell

1.

 +  = _____

_____   _____

2.

 +  = _____

_____   _____

3.

 +  = _____

_____   _____

4.

 +  = _____

_____   _____

Matching Shapes

Directions: Look at the shapes below. Use the Word Bank to help you name each one. Write the name on the line.

Word Bank

cone	cylinder	sphere
cube	rectangular prism	triangular prism

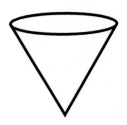

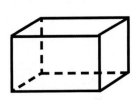

_____ _____ _____

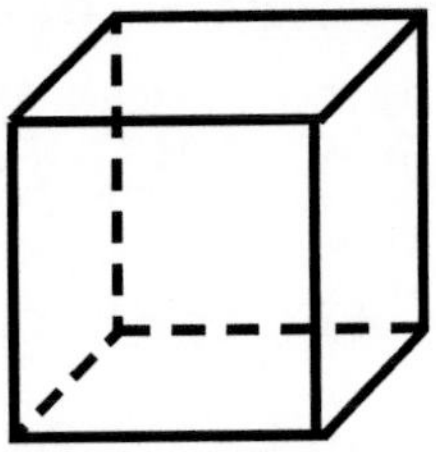

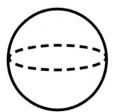

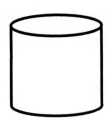

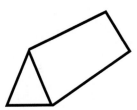

_____ _____ _____

Directions: Draw a line from the objects to the matching shapes above. Use a different color for each shape.

Spelling Practice

Directions: The underlined words are misspelled. Write the correct spelling above each word. Then, rewrite the paragraph using the correct spelling.

When I <u>wuz</u> <u>littl</u>, I did not <u>lik</u> to eat vegetables. My mom <u>woud</u> try <u>vry</u> hard to <u>mak</u> me eat them. <u>Shee</u> <u>sed</u> I needed to eat vegetables so I <u>coold</u> grow strong. I didn't care. I still didn't want to eat <u>thm</u>. Now I am older, and I <u>hav</u> learned to like some vegetables. I <u>wil</u> eat salads and broccoli. <u>Mi</u> mom says <u>shee</u> is proud of me. <u>Wen</u> I grow up, I'm <u>goin</u> to be healthy and strong.

_____

_____

_____

_____

_____

_____

Shape Shirts

Math

Directions: Color the T-shirts that have the same shapes as the first T-shirt.

Directions: Design your own T-shirts, using the shape under each shirt.

circles   rectangles   triangles   squares

Hidden Meaning

Directions: Read each short story. Circle the best answer for each question.

1. Bob wears a wig. He puts on big shoes and silly clothes. Bob paints his face with makeup. Then, he goes to work. What is Bob's job?

    ☼ fireman   ☼ clown   ☼ bus driver

2. Sue could hear meowing. She walked over to the tree and looked up. What was in the tree?

    ☼ a bird   ☼ a dog   ☼ a cat

3. Mom did not want to cook dinner. The doorbell rang. A man was standing there with a thin, square box. What was for dinner?

    ☼ pizza   ☼ an apple   ☼ cereal

4. Mark drew a shape on his paper. He did not lift his pencil at all. The shape had no straight lines. What shape did Mark draw?

    ☼ square   ☼ circle   ☼ triangle

Shapes in Our World

Math

Directions: Read "Shapes in Our World." You will find that some words are missing. Now, reread the story. On the lines, write something in our world that looks like each shape. The first one has been done for you.

Shapes in Our World

Today, I went on a shape hunt with my friends Suzie, Sylvester, and Sam. In

the house, I found a ____table____ that was shaped like a ☐ . I also

found a _____ and a _____ shaped

like a ☐ . Suzie saw a _____ shaped like a △ .

Sylvester looked across the street and saw a _____

shaped like a ⬡ . At the end of the street, Sam saw a _____

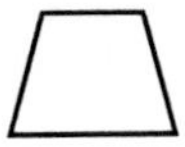

shaped like a ⬡ . We all saw a _____ , a

_____ , and a _____

shaped like a ◯ . We had so much fun that we are going shape-hunting

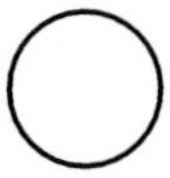

again tomorrow!

Describing Objects

Directions: Write a word from the Word Bank that matches the description in each sentence.

Word Bank

apple pie	fire	shoes	sky
bed	kitten	skateboard	tree

1. The tall, green, leafy _____ was swaying in the wind.

2. The furry, black _____ curled up in the sunshine and slept.

3. I love to eat spicy, warm, delicious, homemade _____ .

4. My _____ goes clickety-clack as I roll down the street.

5. The big, soft, comfy _____ looked great when I was sleepy.

6. These old, dirty, worn-out _____ need to be thrown away.

7. The warm, crackling _____ feels good on a cool night.

8. The beautiful, blue _____ stretched above us.

Swimming Pool

Directions: Finish filling the pool so you and your friends can go swimming. Then, draw your friends swimming in the pool.

Wooden Words

Directions: How many words can you make using the letters in the word "carpenter"?
Write one word on each log below. Look for words that have three or more letters
only! The first one has been done for you.

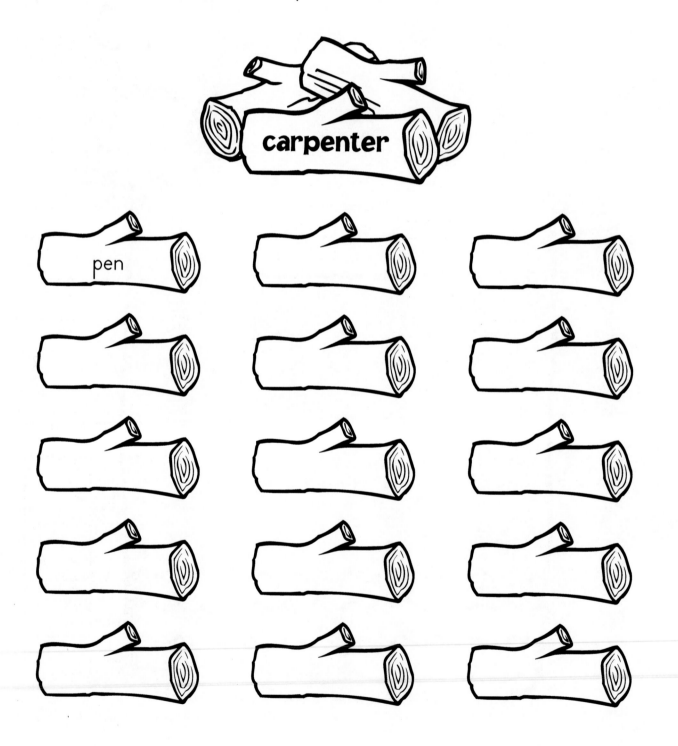

carpenter

pen

Fish Bowl

Directions: Tally the items in the fish bowl. Then, create a bar graph of the tallied information. The first one has been done for you.

Item	Tally Marks
🌿	|
🐌	
🐟	
🐠	

Item	1	2	3	4	5	6	7	8
🌿								
🐌								
🐟								
🐠								

Complete Thoughts

A **sentence** is a complete thought with a subject, a verb, and end punctuation.

Directions: Draw lines to match the groups of words to make sentences. Then, write the sentences on the lines below.

The children	plays the horn.
The man in the band	are having a parade.
I	begins at sunrise.
A new day	hope Grandma can see me.
Everyone	smiles for the picture.

1. _____

   _____

2. _____

   _____

3. _____

   _____

4. _____

   _____

5. _____

   _____

Reading a Graph

Directions: Read this circle graph about where Derek spends the hours in one day. Then, follow the instructions below.

Derek's 24-Hour Day

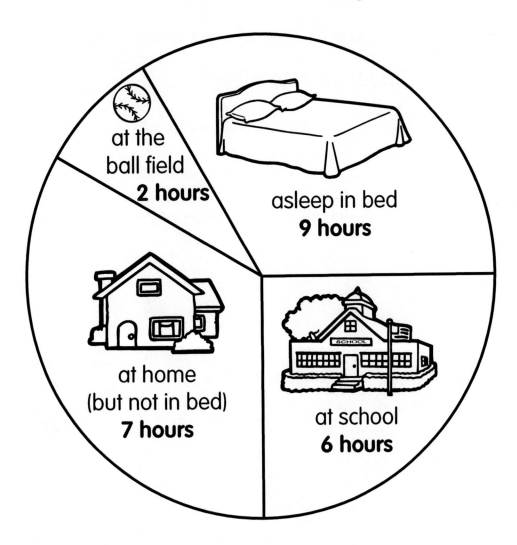

1. Use a **red** crayon to color the place Derek spends six hours a day.

2. Use a **blue** crayon to color Derek's sleeping time.

3. Use a **green** crayon to color the time Derek spends at the ball field.

4. Use a **yellow** crayon to color the time Derek is not sleeping while he is at home.

Switching Sounds

Directions: What happens when you change a sound in a word to another sound? Answer each riddle below.

1. Change the /t/ in **cut** to /p/. What is the new word? _____

2. Change the first /g/ in **giggle** to /w/. What is the new word? _____

3. Change the /m/ in **middle** to /r/. What is the new word? _____

4. Change the /t/ in **chat** to /p/. What is the new word? _____

5. Change the /m/ in **milk** to /s/. What is the new word? _____

6. Change the /u/ in **rug** to /a/. What is the new word? _____

7. Change the /p/ in **picket** to /t/. What is the new word? _____

8. Change the /r/ in **rake** to /c/. What is the new word? _____

9. Change the /b/ in **bow** to /l/. What is the new word? _____

10. Change the /c/ in **crown** to /b/. What is the new word? _____

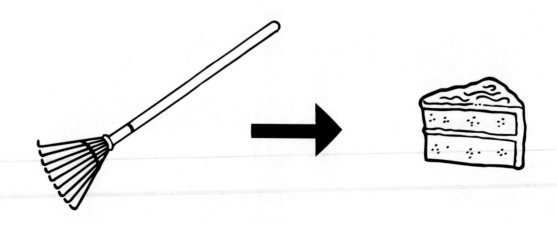

Estimate

Math

Directions: Read each word problem. Circle the better estimate.

1. Tina has a handful of pennies. About how many pennies does Tina have?

7 pennies   70 pennies

2. Shelley has a bowl with a goldfish. About how many goldfish does Shelley have?

1 goldfish   0 goldfish

3. Bill has a bag full of marbles. About how many marbles does Bill have?

2 marbles   20 marbles

4. Tilly has lost some teeth. About how many teeth has Tilly lost?

4 teeth   40 teeth

5. About how long should it take to brush your teeth?

3 seconds   3 minutes   3 hours

6. About how long does it take to bake a cake?

1 second   1 minute   1 hour

Simple Similes

> A **simile** helps a reader "see" objects better. A simile compares two objects using the words *like* or *as*.

Directions: Write a simile for each subject. The first one has been done for you.

1. A teddy bear is

    as _____ soft _____ as _____ a cotton ball _____ .

2. The moon is

    as _____ as _____ .

3. Music is

    as _____ as _____ .

4. A bus is

    as _____ as _____ .

5. The sun is

    as _____ as _____ .

Favorite Subject

Math

Directions: Read the chart, and then answer the questions below.

Our Favorite Subjects	
Subject	**Tally of Votes**
math	|||
art	||||
history		
science	⊬|||
music	||
reading	⊬||	
writing	|||
P.E.	⊬|||
health		

1. What subject is liked the most? _____

2. How many people liked it the most? _____

3. What subjects tied for second place? _____

4. Which subject tied with writing? _____

5. How many more liked math than history? _____

More Than One

> If a word ends in -s, -ss, -x, -z, -sh, or -ch, add -es to make it plural.
> Otherwise, just add -s.

Directions: Rewrite each word in its plural form by writing -s or -es at the end. Use the rule above.

1. box   _____

2. dog   _____

3. brush   _____

4. bench   _____

5. pencil   _____

6. buzz   _____

7. bus   _____

8. glass   _____

9. fox   _____

10. girl   _____

Nice Ride

Directions: Starting at one, connect all the numbers from 1–49. Color the picture when you're done.

Sailing Pirates

Directions: Write a strange story to share with your friends. Fill in the blanks in the box below, but do not look ahead at the story. Then, use the words from the box to complete your strange tale. Read the story to someone you love!

1. month of year _____
2. an illness _____
3. name of a place _____
4. name of a person _____
5. food _____

6. food _____
7. action word _____
8. action word _____
9. name of a thing _____
10. food _____

One cloudy, stormy day in _____ , Frankie woke up with a
                                           1

_____ . His mother made him stay in _____ all day. He fell
        2   3

asleep dreaming about pirates. Suddenly, a loud pirate named _____
                                                                              4

shook him and told him to eat sloppy _____ and hard
                                                        5

_____ for breakfast. Another angry pirate made him
              6

_____ over large pillows and _____ beanbags
        7   8

across his bedroom. A third pirate grabbed him out of bed and made him get on the

great big _____ and sail the high seas. The waves were crashing.
                  9

All of a sudden, Frankie's mom shook him awake. She scared off the mean pirates

and fed him _____ for lunch. He was safe from danger now!
                    10

Draw the Problems

Directions: Follow the steps below to help solve the word problems. Read each problem, and then draw a picture to help solve it.

Solving Word Problems

1. **Read** the word problem a few times.

2. **Underline** the words that give you clues about whether to add, subtract, multiply, or divide.

3. **Draw** a picture to show the solution, or use real items to solve the problem.

4. **Write** the math sentence, and solve the problem.

Breakfast	Lunch

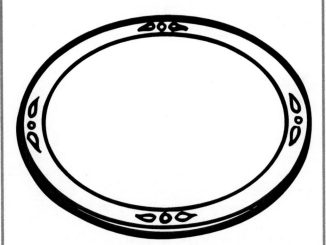

For breakfast, Matt had a bowl of cereal. It had 3 peach slices on it. His mom gave him 5 more peach slices. How many peach slices did he have in all?

For lunch, Matt had a sandwich and 6 carrot sticks on his plate. He ate 5 of the carrot sticks. How many carrot sticks does he have left?

_____

_____

Which Is Best?

Directions: In each row, circle the word that will complete the sentence, and then print it on the line.

1. I was _____ out the window.	**looking** **looked**
2. I _____ it up.	**opening** **opened**
3. The dog _____ in a doghouse.	**living** **lived**
4. My dad _____ French.	**studying** **studied**
5. I was _____ outside.	**playing** **played**
6. My mom was _____ dinner.	**cooking** **cooked**

Just the Facts

Directions: Read the clues. Sometimes you don't need all the information that is given. Practice crossing out what you don't need to solve the problem. Then, write the student's house number on the line.

| 437 | 652 | 743 | 976 |

Sam's House

☼ Sam's house only has one window.

☼ Sam's house number has a 6 in it.

☼ Sam's house has a chimney on the left-hand side.

Sam lives in house number _____.

Ana's House

☼ Ana's house has bushes in the front yard.

☼ Ana's house is large.

☼ Ana's house number has a 6 in it.

Ana lives in house number _____.

David's House

☼ David's house number has a 7 in it.

☼ David's house does not have the highest address on the street.

☼ David's house has a chimney on the right-hand side.

David lives in house number _____.

Mei's House

☼ Mei's house has more than one window.

☼ Mei's house has bushes in the front yard.

☼ Mei's house number has a 3 in the tens place.

Mei lives in house number _____.

End It

Directions: Put the correct punctuation mark in the box at the end of each sentence. Then, identify what kind of sentence has been given by writing *statement, command, question,* or *exclamation* on the line. The first one has been done for you.

1. Triceratops lived long ago [.]

   statement
   _____

2. Was the triceratops the biggest dinosaur [ ]

   _____

3. Wow, that dinosaur looks mean [ ]

   _____

4. Whoa, this museum has a lot of dinosaurs [ ]

   _____

5. Give me the camera [ ]

   _____

6. Where did the triceratops live [ ]

   _____

7. How long was its tail [ ]

   _____

8. Some dinosaurs laid eggs [ ]

   _____

9. Don't touch the bones [ ]

   _____

Missing Piece

Directions: One piece of information is missing from each word problem. Write the missing piece of information on the line. The first one has been done for you.

1. Jewel made 15 cookies. Her dog, Ruby, ate some of them. How many cookies does Jewel have left?

   Missing information: _the number of cookies Ruby ate_

   _____

2. Bart bought 3 books of stamps. Each book has some stamps. How many stamps did Bart buy in all?

   Missing information: _____

   _____

3. Lindsey adopted three animals from the animal shelter. Sara adopted some, too. How many animals were adopted in all?

   Missing information: _____

   _____

4. Larry planted 100 flowers in each of several rows. How many flowers did Larry plant?

   Missing information: _____

   _____

Cacti

Directions: Read the passage, and then answer the questions.

Cacti* grow in places where it does not rain much. When it does rain, their roots get as much water as they can. A cactus can store water for many years. There are more than 2,000 kinds of cacti. Cacti come in many different shapes and sizes. Some cacti are tall and thin. Other cacti are short and round. Cacti have spines instead of leaves. Many cactus spines are very sharp.

Cacti is plural for cactus.

1. Where do cacti grow?

   _____

   _____

2. What do cacti do when it rains?

   _____

   _____

3. How many kinds of cacti are there?

   _____

4. What are some of the shapes and sizes of cacti?

   _____

   _____

5. What do cacti have instead of leaves?

   _____

Add and Subtract

Math

Directions: Read each word problem. Then, write the math problem and the answer. Numbers 1 and 5 have been done for you.

1. Cheryl has 3 goldfish, 4 blue fish, and 6 green fish. How many fish does Cheryl have in all?

   Cheryl has __13__ fish in all.

   ```
      3
      4
   +  6
   ────
     13
   ```

2. Nicole made a headband. She used 7 green feathers, 8 blue feathers, and 1 red feather. How many feathers did Nicole use in all?

   Nicole used _____ feathers in all.

   ```
   +
   ──
   ```

3. Jasmine used beads to make a necklace. She used 6 brown beads, 5 pink beads, and 9 black beads. How many beads did Jasmine use in all?

   Jasmine used _____ beads in all.

   ```
   +
   ──
   ```

4. Angelo likes to play marbles. He has 3 that are cat eyes, 5 that are swirled, and 6 that are solid blue. How many marbles does Angelo have in all?

   Angelo has _____ marbles in all.

   ```
   +
   ──
   ```

5. Paula had 18 seeds. She gave 7 to her sister and 6 to her brother. How many seeds does Paula have left?

   Paula has __5__ seeds left.

   ```
     18
   −  7
   ────
     11
   −  6
   ────
      5
   ```

6. Nick had 15 yo-yos. He lost 3 on his way to school and gave 8 away. How many yo-yos does Nick have left?

   Nick has _____ yo-yos left.

   ```
   −
   ──
   −
   ──
   ```

Action Verbs

Directions: Under each picture below, write two action verbs that describe what you would do there.

1.

_____

_____

2.

_____

_____

3.

_____

_____

4.

_____

_____

5.

_____

_____

6.

_____

_____

Math Wizard

Friday Fun

Directions: Fill in the blank boxes as you follow the path. If the operation says add, add the two numbers together. If it says subtract, take away the second number, and fill in the answer box. The first answer box has been done for you. Get to the end of the path as fast as you can. Can you get through it in one minute?

Start → 5 − 2 = 3 + 1 =

4 + ☐ = 3 − ☐ = 2 +

=

☐ − 1 = ☐ − 2 = +

1

☐ = 1 + ☐ = 4 + ☐ =

−

2 = ☐ − 3 = ☐   Finish!

What's Different?

Directions: There are five things that are different in the second picture. Look at each picture carefully, and find the items that are different. Circle them.

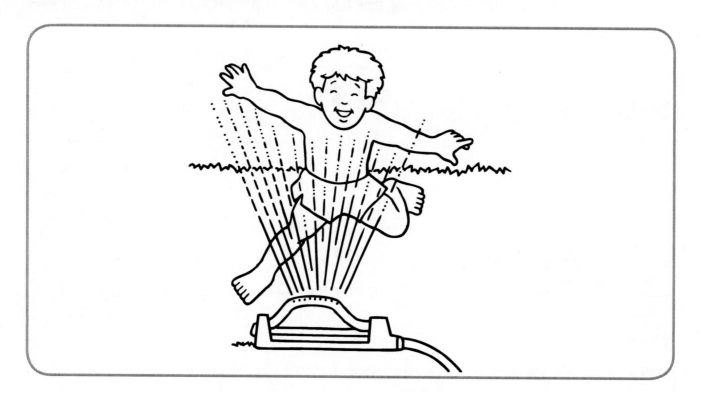

Add Three Numbers

Math

Directions: Read each word problem. Write the number sentence it shows. Then, find the sum.

1.

Kevin went for a walk and saw 1 frog, 3 butterflies, and 5 bugs. How many things did he see in all?

_____ + _____ + _____ = _____

2.

When Sally got on the school bus, there were 8 boys and 10 girls already there. How many children were there on the bus in all?

_____ + _____ + _____ = _____

3.

John ate a pizza with 7 mushrooms, 6 olives, and 5 pieces of pepperoni. How many toppings were on his pizza in all?

_____ + _____ + _____ = _____

4.

Today, Jan saw 3 birds, 2 dogs, and 5 puppies in the park. How many animals did she see in all?

_____ + _____ + _____ = _____

Find the Adjectives

Directions: Adjectives are describing words. They describe nouns and pronouns. Read the passage below, and circle all of the adjectives. Then, use the adjectives to answer the questions below.

Every day I wake up to the noise of the neighbor's dog, Cuddles, scratching at my door. Cuddles seems like she would be a great dog, but she is not. Cuddles is a tiny dog, no taller than my shin. She is a miniature poodle with white fur. She is also a very mean, bossy, and loud dog. You may think that I am just a grouchy kid, but I am not. For some reason, Cuddles comes to the back door of my house and wants me to feed her. Her owner is hard of hearing and can't hear Cuddles and her barking. One morning, when I heard Cuddles, I made the mistake of getting up to see what she wanted. My mom thinks it should be my job to help out. Now, don't get me wrong, I like to help out when I can. But can I help at some time other than five o'clock in the morning?

1. What kind of dog is Cuddles? _____

2. What color fur does Cuddles have? _____

3. What size is Cuddles? _____

4. How does the author describe Cuddles? _____

5. Why doesn't the owner feed Cuddles? _____

   _____

6. What kind of kid does the author think you will consider him or her to be?

   _____

7. At which door does Cuddles wait? _____

More Time Practice

Directions: Read the problems. Write the correct ending time on the lines, and then draw hands on each clock to show that time.

1. The play began at 6:00 and lasted half an hour. What time did the play end?

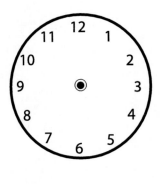

_____ : _____ _____

2. The school bus picked us up at 2:00. The bus ride took half an hour. What time did we get home?

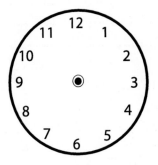

_____ : _____ _____

3. We went to the park at 4:00. We played for half an hour. What time did we leave the park?

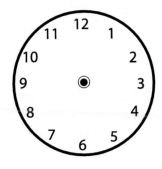

_____ : _____ _____

4. The baby fell asleep at 9:00 and napped for half an hour. What time did the baby wake up?

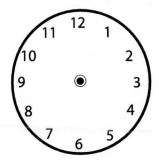

_____ : _____ _____

The Bossy Rr

When an *r* follows a vowel, it controls the vowel, making it sound different from the usual long or short sounds.

Directions: Use the words from the Word Bank to help write the names of each picture below. Then, look for the *r*-controlled vowels, and sort the words into the correct columns on the chart.

Word Bank

corn   horse   purse   shark   star   turkey

1. _____

2. _____

3. _____

4. _____

5. _____

6. _____

ar	or	ur

©Teacher Created Resources, Inc.

Story Problems

Math

Directions: Read and solve each word problem.

1. Lucas planted a seed. It grew 1 inch every day for a week. How tall is the plant?

   The plant is _____ inches tall.

2. Betsy is 38 inches tall. Her brother is 6 inches shorter. How tall is her brother?

   Betsy's brother is _____ inches tall.

3. Theodore's snake was 15 inches long. It grew 1 inch a month for the next 3 months. How long is Theodore's snake?

   Theodore's snake is _____ inches long.

4. Jason had a piece of yarn. He cut it into 2 pieces. Each piece was 6 inches long. How long was the piece of yarn before Jason cut it?

   Jason's piece of yarn was _____ inches long.

5. Penny's zinnias are 5 inches tall. The tulips are twice as tall as the zinnias. How tall are the tulips?

   The tulips are _____ inches tall.

6. Last year, Andrew grew 4 inches. This year, he is 35 inches tall. How tall was Andrew last year?

   Andrew was _____ inches tall.

What Is It?

Directions: Use your imagination to finish the picture below. When your picture is finished, write a story about what you have created.

_____

_____

_____

_____

_____

_____

Mystery Number

Directions: Use the hundreds chart to solve each problem.

1. I am larger than 20 and less than 40. I am an even number. When you count by tens, you say my name.

   What number am I? _____

2. I am less than 80 but larger than 10. I have two numbers that are the same. My two numbers added together equal 4.

   What number am I? _____

3. I am larger than 50 and less than 100. I have a 5 in the ones place. I have a number smaller than 6 in the tens place.

   What number am I? _____

4. I have a 2 as one of my numbers. When you count by tens, you say my name.

   What number am I? _____

1	2	3	4	5	6	7	8	9	10
11	12	13	14	15	16	17	18	19	20
21	22	23	24	25	26	27	28	29	30
31	32	33	34	35	36	37	38	39	40
41	42	43	44	45	46	47	48	49	50
51	52	53	54	55	56	57	58	59	60
61	62	63	64	65	66	67	68	69	70
71	72	73	74	75	76	77	78	79	80
81	82	83	84	85	86	87	88	89	90
91	92	93	94	95	96	97	98	99	100

Do You Know?

Directions: Pay close attention to the details, and see if you can predict what will happen next by circling the correct answer.

1. Andy wants to hit a home run at his next baseball game. Every day he practices baseball with his dad. Each day he hits the ball better and better. Before the game begins, Andy feels sure he can hit a home run.

   What do you think will happen at the game?

   ☼ Andy will tell the coach he doesn't want to play.

   ☼ Andy will play very well during the game.

2. Maria and her brother Carl are both taking swimming lessons during the summer. Maria likes the water and is excited about the lessons. Carl is afraid of the water, but his swimming teacher is patient and nice. She tells Carl that each day he will learn a little more than the day before. By the third day, Carl is no longer afraid to get into the pool.

   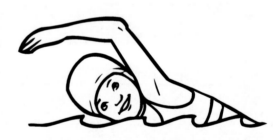

   What do you think will happen next?

   ☼ Carl will learn how to swim.

   ☼ Maria will stop wanting to take swimming lessons.

Action!

Directions: Look at the verbs in the Word Bank. Then, find and circle these words in the puzzle below.

Word Bank

BUILD	JUMP	RUN
CATCH	LAUGH	SKIP
CLIMB	LISTEN	SLIDE
COUGH	LOOK	SMILE
EAT	PAINT	SWIM
HOP	PLAY	THROW
JOG	READ	YAWN

B	P	F	M	S	K	C	S	I	Q	P	L
E	M	I	H	P	U	A	O	M	U	E	I
P	W	I	A	O	A	T	E	D	I	L	S
S	J	I	L	N	P	C	K	K	D	L	T
N	N	U	U	C	T	H	R	O	W	D	E
T	E	R	M	H	F	G	G	S	Z	L	N
N	E	T	G	P	P	U	X	K	R	I	Z
U	W	U	I	L	C	O	F	I	A	U	V
V	A	A	A	L	U	C	K	P	G	B	T
L	Y	Y	Y	E	A	T	T	S	O	N	E
E	R	G	B	E	P	U	R	Z	J	T	Y
K	O	O	L	V	R	E	A	D	W	C	E

Fishy, Fishy

Directions: Can you find all eight hidden objects? Circle each object as you find it, and cross out the word in the box.

Hidden Objects			
candy bar	French fries	hamburger	sub sandwich
chicken leg	grilled cheese sandwich	soda can	taco

All About Me

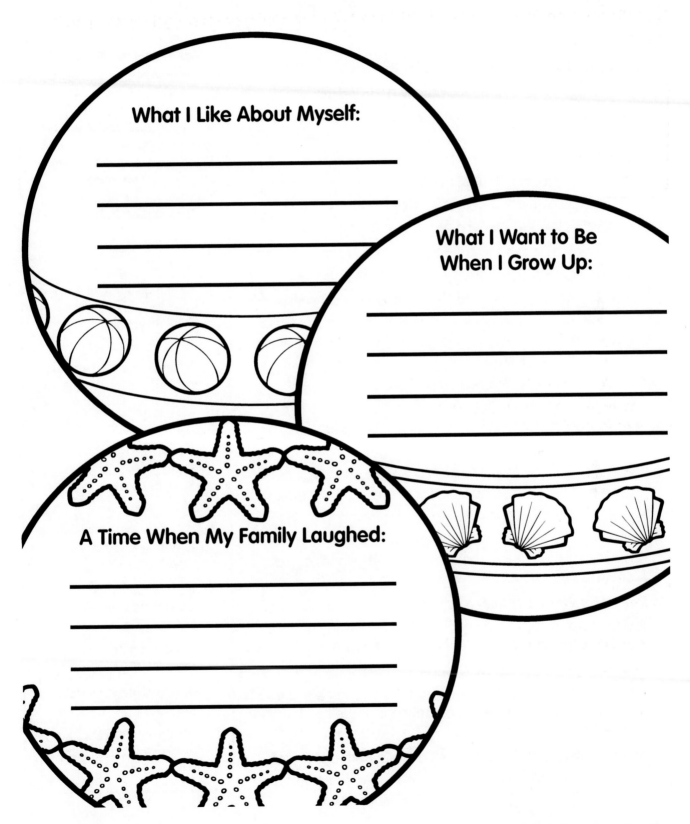

What I Like About Myself:

_____

_____

_____

_____

**What I Want to Be
When I Grow Up:**

_____

_____

_____

_____

A Time When My Family Laughed:

_____

_____

_____

_____

Summer Reading List

○ **The Pot That Juan Built** by Nancy Andrews-Goebel

This is the story of Juan Quezada who rediscovered the art of pottery-making as it was practiced by ancient peoples of Mexico and led to the revitalization of the village of Mata Ortiz.

○ **Castles, Caves, and Honeycombs** by Linda Ashman

This book describes the unique places where animals build their homes.

○ **My Light** by Molly Bang

This book is about the journey of light from the sun to Earth and how it is connected to many different types of energy.

○ **Knockin' on Wood: Starring Peg Leg Bates** by Lynne Barasch

Even though he lost his leg in an unfortunate factory accident, Clayton "Peg Leg" Bates became a famous tap dancer.

○ **Forest Explorer: A Life-sized Field Guide** by Nic Bishop

This book has detailed photos of several different deciduous forest habitats, including field notes about insects and animals that live in those habitats.

○ **One Small Place by the Sea** by Barbara Brenner

This book offers an up-close look at tide-pool life, including how its creatures and plants are all interconnected.

○ **Jim Thorpe's Bright Path** by Joseph Bruchac

This is a biography about the Native American athlete Jim Thorpe and the path he had to take to fame and Olympic gold.

○ **Bob** by Tracey Campbell Pearson

A rooster trying to learn how to crow ends up learning how to sound like many different animals. His verbal abilities help save lives when he scares away a fox.

○ **Diary of a Worm** by Doreen Cronin

A young worm keeps a diary about his day-to-day activities and the not-so-good things about being a worm.

○ **Birdbrain Amos** by Michael Delaney

A hippo named Amos places an ad for a bird to help him with a bug problem, but he gets more than he bargained for when a bird answers his ad.

○ **Muncha! Muncha! Muncha!** by Candace Fleming

Enjoy this onomatopoeic romp through a vegetable garden with a troublesome trio of smart cottontail bunnies.

Making the Most of Summertime Reading

When reading these books with your child, you may wish to ask the questions below. The sharing of questions and answers will enhance and improve your child's reading comprehension skills.

○ Why did you pick this book to read?

○ Name a character from the story that you like. Why do you like him or her?

○ Where does the story take place? Do you want to go there?

○ Name a problem from the story. How is it solved?

○ What is the best part of the story so far? Describe it!

○ What do you think is going to happen next in the story? Guess!

○ Who are the important characters in the story? Why are they important?

○ What is the book about?

○ What are two things you have learned by reading this book?

○ Would you tell your friend to read this book? Why or why not?

Summer Reading List

- **Roller Coaster** by Marla Frazee

  Characters set aside their fears and ride a roller coaster.

- **Bluebird Summer** by Deborah Hopkinson

  When a grandmother passes away, her grandchildren work to restore the garden she loved.

- **Henry Climbs a Mountain** by D. B. Johnson

  In this story, Henry willingly goes to jail rather than sacrifice his values despite his love for freedom.

- **Isabel's House of Butterflies** by Tony Johnston

  Isabel, an eight-year-old girl, devises a plan that will save her favorite tree, bring the monarch butterflies back, and help bring money home for her family.

- **Farfallina & Marcel** by Holly Keller

  A caterpillar meets a baby goose, and they become good friends. They both transform after some time passes and miss each other, only to be reunited as a grown butterfly and gray goose.

- **How I Became a Pirate** by Melinda Long

  The main character, Jeremy, is needed by a band of pirates because he is a good digger, but he soon misses the comforts of home.

- **Moses Goes to the Circus** by Isaac Millman

  Moses, who is deaf, has fun with his family at a circus, where they communicate via sign language.

- **Mice and Beans** by Pam Munoz Ryan

  Rosa Maria tries to trap mice, who she thinks are stealing from her, only to discover how helpful they really are.

- **The Day the Babies Crawled Away** by Peggy Rathmann

  A boy saves several babies who crawled away while their parents were occupied.

- **The Island-below-the-Star** by James Rumford

  In this folktale adventure, five brothers set out in a canoe to find the island (now known as Hawaii) below the star.

- **A Bad Case of Stripes** by David Shannon

  Camilla Cream has come down with a mysterious ailment—stripes! Can anyone help her?

- **Chato and the Party Animals** by Gary Soto

  Chato the Cat plans a surprise party for his best friend but realizes he forgot to invite the guest of honor!

- **Mary Smith** by Andrea U'Ren

  Before alarm clocks were invented, Mary Smith woke up her neighbors by shooting peas at their windows.

- **Don't Let the Pigeon Drive the Bus!** by Mo Willems

  A pigeon wants desperately to drive the bus and tries his best to convince the driver to let him.

Fun Ways to Love Books

Here are some fun ways that your child can expand on his or her reading. Most of these ideas will involve both you and your child; however, the wording has been directed towards your child because we want him or her to be inspired to love books.

Design a Bookmark

You can design a bookmark for your favorite book, and then use it in other books to remind you of a great reading experience. Use a strip of colorful paper and include the title, the author, and a picture of something that happened in the book.

Book Chain

Create a book chain to link your favorite books together. First, cut out strips of colored paper. On one, write down the name of your favorite book. On the other, describe your favorite part of the story. Staple or tape the strips of paper together to form a circle. Do this for each book you read, and link all of your books together. Use the chain to decorate your room.

A Comic Book

Turn your favorite book into a comic book. Fold at least two sheets of paper in half, and staple them so they make a book. With a ruler and pencil, draw boxes across each page to look like blank comic strips. Then, draw the story of your book as if it were a comic. Draw pictures of your characters, and have words coming out of their mouths—just as in a real comic strip.

Novel Foods

What foods do the characters in your book eat? What do they drink? What are their favorite foods? Get a better sense of your characters' tastes by cooking their favorite foods. Some characters love sweet things, like cookies and ice cream. Other characters like hamburgers and pizza. Decide what foods your characters love. With your parents' help, locate appropriate recipes on the Internet or in books. Then, make up a grocery list. Buy groceries and gather necessary materials, such as mixing bowls, spoons, and pans. Cook your characters' favorite foods by yourself or with friends.

Story Time for Pets

Some cats and dogs enjoy being read to. They appreciate the verbal attention—especially if it's accompanied by a loving scratch behind the ears. Choose your favorite book, and read it to your pet. Notice whether he or she particularly likes being read to. Your dog may tilt its head and raise its ears, trying to understand what you are reading. A cat may rub its cheek against you or climb into your lap as you read. You might even want to read a special book about a dog or cat to your pet.

Bookmark Your Words

Reading Log

Make summertime reading lots of fun with these reading log glasses. Have your child fill in the glasses after his or her daily reading. For younger children, you may need to help them fill in the information. Or, as an alternative, they can draw a picture of something they read from that day. Once they have completed the glasses, they can cut them out and use them as bookmarks.

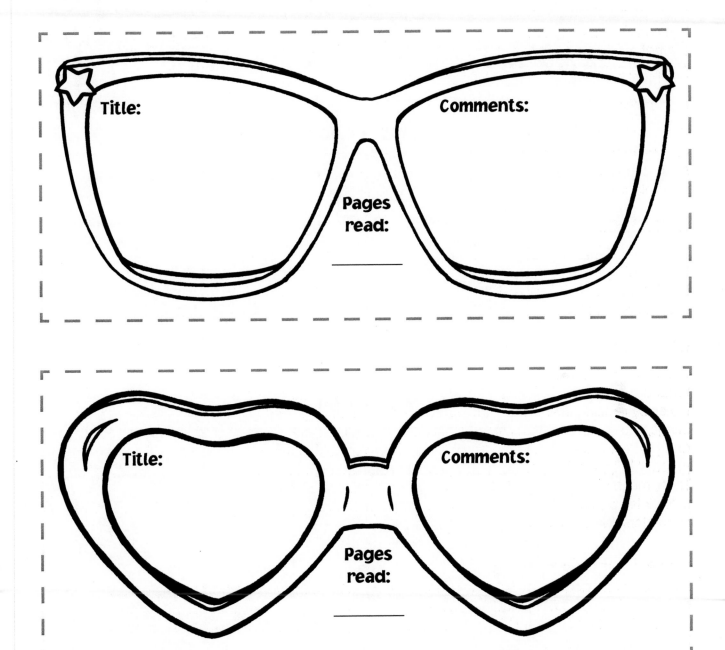

This page may be reproduced as many times as needed.

Read-Together Chart

Does your father read books to you before bed? Perhaps your mother reads to the family at breakfast? Your grandparents may enjoy reading books to you after school or on the weekends. You and your family members can create a Read-Together Chart and fill it in to keep track of all the books you've read together.

Here are two Read-Together Charts. The first one is a sample. The second one has been left blank, so you can add your own categories and books.

Sample Chart

Book We Read	Who Read It?	Summary	Our Review
The Secret Garden	My older sister read it to me.	It's about a spoiled girl who learns to love nature and people.	We like this book. The characters are funny, and the illustrations are beautiful!

Your Chart

This page may be reproduced as many times as needed.

Journal Topics

Choose one of these journal topics each day. Make sure you add enough detail so someone reading this will clearly be able to know at least four of the following:

☼ **who**   ☼ **what**   ☼ **when**   ☼ **where**   ☼ **why**   ☼ **how**

1. I like (or dislike) my name because . . .
2. My favorite thing to do in the summer is . . .
3. The hardest thing I've ever had to do was . . .
4. My favorite toy or stuffed animal is . . .
5. My bedroom is special because . . .
6. My favorite thing about being in first grade was . . .
7. The thing I'm most looking forward to in second grade is . . .
8. If I had $100.00, I would . . .
9. If I could fly, I would . . .
10. The kind of books I like to read are . . .
11. When I grow up, I want to be . . .
12. If I were President of the United States, I would . . .
13. I can tell someone is kind when . . .
14. My favorite kind of music is . . .
15. I want to know more about . . .
16. I wish I could . . .
17. The biggest mess I ever made was . . .
18. At the park, I like to . . .
19. If I were any kind of animal, I would be . . .
20. The best day I ever had was . . .
21. The worst day I ever had was . . .
22. I would like to meet . . .
23. My favorite thing to eat for dinner is . . .
24. My family helps me . . .
25. The funniest thing I've ever seen is . . .

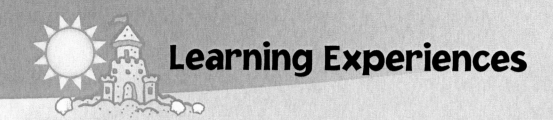

Learning Experiences

Here are some fun, low-cost activities that you can do with your child. You'll soon discover that these activities can be stimulating, educational, and complementary to the other exercises in this book.

Flash Cards

Make up all types of flash cards. Depending on your child's interests and grade level, these cards might feature enrichment words, math problems, or states and capitals. You can create them yourself with markers or on a computer. Let your child help cut pictures out of magazines and glue them on. Then, find a spot outdoors, and go through the flash cards with your child.

Project Pantry

Find a spot in your house where you can store supplies. This might be a closet or a bin that stays in one spot. Get some clean paint cans or buckets. Fill them with all types of craft and art supplies. Besides the typical paints, markers, paper, scissors, and glue, include some more unusual things, such as tiles, artificial flowers, and wrapping paper. This way, whenever you and your child want to do a craft project, you have everything you need at that moment.

The Local Library

Check out everything that your local library has to offer. Most libraries offer summer reading programs with various incentives. Spend an afternoon choosing and then reading books together.

Collect Something

Let your child choose something to collect that is free or inexpensive, such as paper clips or buttons. If your child wants to collect something that might be impractical like horses, find pictures in magazines or catalogs, and have your child cut them out and start a picture collection.

Grocery Store Trip

Instead of making a trip to the grocery store a chore, make it a challenge. Even with nonreaders, you can have them help you find items on the shelf. Start by giving your child a list of his or her own. Review the list before you go. For nonreaders, you might want to cut pictures from ads. Many stores even have smaller shopping carts, so your child can have his or her own cart to fill. Once you get to an aisle where you know there is something on your child's list, prompt him or her to find the item. You may have to help your child get something down from a shelf.

Eating the Alphabet

Wouldn't it be fun to eat the alphabet? During the course of the summer, see how many fresh fruits and vegetables you can eat from A to Z. You and your child can make a poster or a chart with the letters A–Z on it. Once you have the chart, each time your child eats a fruit or vegetable, write it next to the matching letter of the alphabet. You can also let your child draw a picture of what he or she has eaten.

Learning Experiences
(cont.)

How Much Does It Cost?

If you go out for a meal, have your child help total the bill. Write down the cost of each person's meal. Then, have your child add them all together. You can vary this and make it much simpler by having your child just figure out the cost of an entrée and a drink or the cost of three desserts. You might want to round the figures first.

Nature Scavenger Hunt

Take a walk, go to a park, or hike in the mountains. But before you go, create a scavenger hunt list for your child. This can consist of all sorts of things found in nature. Make sure your child has a bag to carry everything he or she finds. (Be sure to check ahead of time about the rules or laws regarding removing anything.) You might include things like a leaf with pointed edges, a speckled rock, and a twig with two small limbs on it. Take a few minutes to look at all the things your child has collected, and check them off the list.

Measure It!

Using a ruler, tape measure, or yardstick is one way to see how tall something is. Start with your child, and find out how tall he or she is. Now, find other things to measure and compare. Find out how much shorter a book is compared to your child, or discover how much taller the door is than your child. To measure things that can't be measured with a ruler, take some string and stretch it around the object. Cut or mark it where it ends. Then, stretch the string next to the ruler or tape measure to find out how long it is. Your child may be surprised at how different something that is the same number of inches looks when the shape is different.

Take a Trip, and Keep a Journal

If you are going away during the summer, have your child keep a journal. Depending on his or her age, this can take a different look. A young child can collect postcards and paste them into a blank journal. He or she can also draw pictures of places he or she is visiting. An older child can keep a traditional journal and draw pictures. Your child can also do a photo-journal if a camera is available for him or her to use.

Be a Scientist

Without your child's knowledge, put a ball inside a box, and cover it with a lid. Call in your child, and tell him or her to act like a scientist. He or she will need to ask questions and try to figure out answers like a scientist would. If your child is having a hard time asking questions, you may need to help. Some questions to ask include, "What do you think is inside the box?" and "How do you know?" Have your child shake the box and see if he or she can figure it out.

Web Sites

Math Web Sites

☼ **AAA Math:** http://www.aaamath.com
This site contains hundreds of pages of basic math skills divided by grade or topic.

☼ **AllMath.com:** http://www.allmath.com
This site has math flashcards, biographies of mathematicians, and a math glossary.

☼ **BrainBashers:** http://www.brainbashers.com
This is a unique collection of brainteasers, games, and optical illusions.

☼ **Coolmath.com:** http://www.coolmath.com
Explore this amusement park of mathematics! Have fun with the interactive activities.

☼ **Mrs. Glosser's Math Goodies:** http://www.mathgoodies.com
This is a free educational Web site featuring interactive worksheets, puzzles, and more!

Reading and Writing Web Sites

☼ **Aesop's Fables:** http://www.umass.edu/aesop
This site has almost forty of the fables. Both traditional and modern versions are presented.

☼ **American Library Association:** http://ala.org
Visit this site to find out both the past and present John Newbery Medal and Randolph Caldecott Medal winners.

☼ **Book Adventure:** http://www.bookadventure.com
This site features a free reading incentive program dedicated to encouraging children in grades K–8 to read.

☼ **Chateau Meddybemps—Young Writers Workshop:** http://www.meddybemps.com/9.700.html
Use the provided story starters to help your child write a story.

☼ **Fairy Godmother:** http://www.fairygodmother.com
This site will capture your child's imagination and spur it on to wonderful creativity.

☼ **Grammar Gorillas:** http://www.funbrain.com/grammar
Play grammar games on this site that proves that grammar can be fun!

☼ **Graphic Organizers:** http://www.eduplace.com/graphicorganizer
Use these graphic organizers to help your child write in an organized manner.

☼ **Rhymezone:** http://www.rhymezone.com
Type in the word you want to rhyme. If there is a rhyming word to match your word, you'll find it here.

☼ **Storybook:** http://www.kids-space.org/story/story.html
Storybook takes children's stories and publishes them on this Web site. Just like in a library, children can choose a shelf and read stories.

Web Sites (cont.)

Reading and Writing Web Sites (cont.)

☼ **Wacky Web Tales:** http://www.eduplace.com/tales/index.html
This is a great place for budding writers to submit their stories and read other children's writing.

☼ **Write on Reader:** http://library.thinkquest.org/J001156
Children can visit Write on Reader to gain a love of reading and writing.

General Web Sites

☼ **Animal Photos:** http://nationalzoo.si.edu
This site offers wonderful pictures of animals, as well as virtual zoo visits.

☼ **Animal Planet:** http://animal.discovery.com
Best for older kids, children can watch videos or play games at this site for animal lovers.

☼ **Congress for Kids:** http://www.congressforkids.net
Children can go to this site to learn all about the branches of the United States government.

☼ **Dinosaur Guide:** http://dsc.discovery.com/dinosaurs
This is an interactive site on dinosaurs that goes beyond just learning about the creatures.

☼ **The Dinosauria:** http://www.ucmp.berkeley.edu/diapsids/dinosaur.html
This site focuses on dispelling dinosaur myths. Read about fossils, history, and more.

☼ **Earthquake Legends:** http://www.fema.gov/kids/eqlegnd.htm
On this site, children can read some of the tales behind earthquakes that people of various cultures once believed.

☼ **The Electronic Zoo:** http://netvet.wustl.edu/e-zoo.htm
This site has links to thousands of animal sites covering every creature under the sun!

☼ **Great Buildings Online:** http://www.greatbuildings.com
This gateway to architecture around the world and across history documents a thousand buildings and hundreds of leading architects.

☼ **Maggie's Earth Adventures:** http://www.missmaggie.org
Join Maggie and her dog, Dude, on a wonderful Earth adventure.

☼ **Mr. Dowling's Electronic Passport:** http://www.mrdowling.com/index.html
This is an incredible history and geography site.

☼ **Sesame Street:** http://www.sesamestreet.org
There is no shortage of fun for children at Sesame Street.

☼ **Tropical Twisters:** http://kids.mtpe.hq.nasa.gov/archive/hurricane/index.html
Take an in-depth look at hurricanes, from how they're created to how dangerous they are.

Printing Chart

Addition Chart

+	0	1	2	3	4	5	6	7	8	9
0	0	1	2	3	4	5	6	7	8	9
1	1	2	3	4	5	6	7	8	9	10
2	2	3	4	5	6	7	8	9	10	11
3	3	4	5	6	7	8	9	10	11	12
4	4	5	6	7	8	9	10	11	12	13
5	5	6	7	8	9	10	11	12	13	14
6	6	7	8	9	10	11	12	13	14	15
7	7	8	9	10	11	12	13	14	15	16
8	8	9	10	11	12	13	14	15	16	17
9	9	10	11	12	13	14	15	16	17	18

Clock Pattern

Use this clock pattern to practice telling time. Ask your parents to photocopy this page and cut out the hour and minute hands below. Then, have them attach the hands to the center dot on the clock's face using a brad (paper fastener). Or, as an alternative, you can use a small paper clip for the hour hand and a large paper clip for the minute hand.

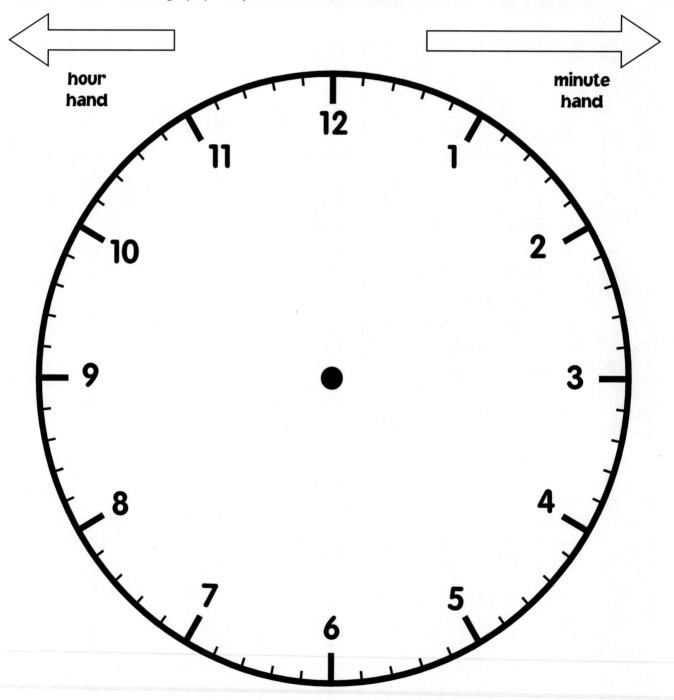

This page may be reproduced as many times as needed.

Measurement Tools

Measurement Conversion Chart

	cups (c.)	1	2	4	8	16
	pints (pt.)	$\frac{1}{2}$	1	2	4	8
	quarts (qt.)	$\frac{1}{4}$	$\frac{1}{2}$	1	2	4
	gallons (gal.)	$\frac{1}{16}$	$\frac{1}{8}$	$\frac{1}{4}$	$\frac{1}{2}$	1

Inch Ruler Cutout

Directions: Cut out the two ruler parts, and tape them together.

Centimeter Ruler Cutout

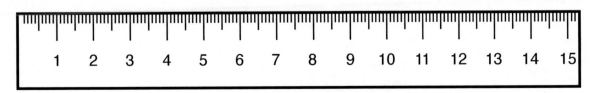

This page may be reproduced as many times as needed.

Answer Key

Page 11

2. 5 tens, 7 ones, 57
3. 9 tens, 3 ones, 93
4. 5 tens, 0 ones, 50
5. 6 tens, 5 ones, 65
6. 2 tens, 1 one, 21

Page 12

1. **bag**
2. **sun**
3. **bug**
4. **fan**
5. **moon**
6. **web**
7. **jet**
8. **bib**
9. **bat**
10. **jeep**
11. **cup** or **mug**
12. **gum**

Page 13

Answers will vary. Possible answers:

2. 1 dime, 1 penny; 2 nickels, 1 penny; 1 nickel, 6 pennies; 11 pennies
3. 2 dimes, 1 nickel; 5 nickels; 3 nickels, 1 dime; 4 nickels, 5 pennies; 25 pennies; 1 quarter
4. 2 quarters; 5 dimes; 10 nickels; 50 pennies; 1 quarter, 2 dimes, 1 nickel; 1 half dollar
5. 6 pennies; 1 nickel, 1 penny
6. 15 pennies; 1 dime, 1 nickel; 3 nickels; 1 dime, 5 pennies; 2 nickels, 5 pennies

Page 14

2. **T**he beach is a fun place to go in **J**uly.
3. **D**id you see that bird fly over **J**essica's head**?**
4. **M**y friend **J**ulian and **I** like to ride the waves.
5. **L**ook out for that foaming, white wave**!**
6. **W**hat can you find at the beach in **A**ugust**?**
7. **A**t the beach**,** **I** saw sand**,** seaweed**,** and rocks.
8. **O**n **S**unday, a big**,** orange crab crawled across my towel.

Page 15

1. **>**, **63** is greater than **42**.
2. **>**, **19** is greater than **16**.
3. **<**, **21** is less than **31**.
4. **>**, **100** is greater than **10**.
5. **=**, **80** is equal to **80**.
6. **<**, **15** is less than **51**.

Page 16

Answers will vary.

Page 17

Make sure that the chart is filled in correctly.

1. Red: 70, 80, 90, 100
2. Yellow circle: 61, 62, 63, 64, 65, 66, 67, 68, 69
3. Green square: 66, 77, 88, 99
4. Blue star: 63, 73, 83, 93
5. Purple line: 67, 70, 71, 72, 73, 74, 75, 76, 77, 78, 79, 87, 97

Page 18

Sentences will vary; possible verbs are as follows:

2. point
3. crawl
4. yell
5. kick

Page 19

Make sure that the gumballs are colored correctly.

Page 20

The word "FROM" is not in the bowl of soup.

Page 21

1. 12
2. 14
3. 18
4. 15
5. 18
6. 7
7. 12
8. 13
9. 16
10. 11

Answer Key (cont.)

Page 22

2. . 4. ? 6. . 8. .

3. . 5. . 7. ?

Page 23

1. 1 6. 10
2. 5 7. 7
3. 4 8. 0
4. 3 9. 8
5. 2 10. 6

Answer: To get to the other slide.

Page 24

2. went, dent
3. bun, fun
4. like, hike
5. boat, coat
6. heat, seat
7. bake, wake
8. wig, fig
9. nose, hose
10. fog or frog, log

Page 25

1. 16 11. 16
2. 14 12. 15
3. 14 13. 18
4. 15 14. 17
5. 17 15. 13
6. 12 16. 3
7. 15 17. 10
8. 17 18. 6
9. 18 19. 12
10. 14

Page 26

My sister is funny:
    She wears strange clothes.
    My sister even dyed her hair blue.

I love to watch my mom cook:
    Everything she makes smells so good.
    Sometimes she lets me lick the bowl.
    She gives me little bites of my favorite foods.

Page 27

1. 39
2. 47
3. 52
4. 72
5. 24
6. 27

Secret number: 27

Page 28

Answers will vary.

Page 29

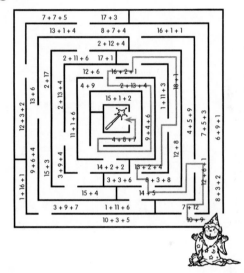

Page 30

Possible answers: tree, fruit, sky, vane, snake, hay, gate, door, rake, hoe, wheel, horse, sheep, goat, seeds, pail

Page 31

2. $7 - 5 = 2$
3. $9 - 2 = 7$
4. $10 - 4 = 6$
5. $5 - 0 = 5$

Page 32

f: fall, gift, leaf
m: milk, camel, gum
n: nut, tent, rain
p: play, apple, cup
s: sack, vest, eggs

Answer Key *(cont.)*

Page 33

1. 5, blue	9. 1, blue
2. 1, blue	10. 2, red
3. 5, blue	11. 2, red
4. 5, blue	12. 3, blue
5. 3, blue	13. 3, blue
6. 2, red	14. 3, blue
7. 4, red	15. 3, blue
8. 3, blue	16. 1, blue

Page 34

2. performers, theater, song

3. children, pool, bathing suits

4. queen, castle, crown

5. boy, library, book

Page 35

1. $11 - 3 = $ **8** (color), $18 - 10 = $ **8** (color), $13 - 7 = $ **6**, $17 - 3 = $ **14**, $20 - 12 = $ **8** (color)

2. $19 - 8 = $ **11** (color), $14 - 5 = $ **9**, $13 - 3 = $ **10**, $20 - 9 = $ **11** (color), $17 - 6 = $ **11** (color)

3. $17 - 7 = $ **10** (color), $19 - 9 = $ **10** (color), $15 - 6 = $ **9**, $14 - 4 = $ **10** (color), $11 - 2 = $ **9**

4. $20 - 13 = $ **7**, $18 - 12 = $ **6** (color), $19 - 4 = $ **15**, $13 - 7 = $ **6** (color), $17 - 11 = $ **6** (color)

Page 36

Today, my grandma took me to the pet store. At the pet store, Grandma said I could get a pet. I picked out a bird. I named it Bailey. After she paid for the bird, I could not wait to get Bailey home. We definitely had a wonderful day at the pet store!

Page 37

1. 6	7. 18
2. 9	8. 5
3. 13	9. 9
4. 10	10. 7
5. 7	11. 23
6. 19	12. 11

Page 38

Answers will vary.

Page 39

Gray (the whale):

$15 - 11 = 4$

$18 - 12 = 6$

$17 - 12 = 5$

$18 - 15 = 3$

$18 - 11 = 7$

$18 - 13 = 5$

$18 - 9 = 9$

$17 - 11 = 6$

$17 - 10 = 7$

Blue (area around the whale):

$17 - 2 = 15$

$18 - 5 = 13$

$17 - 6 = 11$

$17 - 1 = 16$

$18 - 3 = 15$

$18 - 6 = 12$

$18 - 7 = 11$

$17 - 5 = 12$

$17 - 3 = 14$

$18 - 4 = 14$

$17 - 4 = 13$

$18 - 2 = 16$

Page 40

1. bed

2. lamp

3. oven

4. television

5. table

6. sink

7. glass

8. chair

9. towel

10. spoon

Answer Key *(cont.)*

Page 41
2. 1, 3, 2
3. 2, 3, 1
4. 3, 1, 2
6. <
7. <
8. >

Page 42
2. didn't, did not
3. I've, I have
4. I'm, I am
5. you're, you are
6. wouldn't, would not
7. let's, let us
8. she's, she is
9. we're, we are
10. here's, here is

Page 43
2. 1
3. 4
4. 1
5. 3
6. 5

Page 44
Additional words will vary. Circled words are as follows:
2. shells
3. cherry
4. think
5. shoes
6. duck
7. chair
8. whistle
9. wick
10. shuttle

Page 45
1. left pot
2. right box
3. right mug
4. right bowl
5. left bucket
6. left jug
7. right trash can
8. right basket

Page 46
Answers will vary. Possible answers:
1. shiny, red
2. shy, little
3. beautiful, furry
4. big, crisp
5. fast, black
6. loud, blue

Page 47
2. 10:30; little hand between the 10 and 11, big hand on the 6
3. 2:30; little hand between the 2 and 3, big hand on the 6
4. 4:30; little hand between the 4 and 5, big hand on the 6
5. 1:30; little hand between the 1 and 2, big hand on the 6
6. 12:30; little hand between the 12 and 1, big hand on the 6

Page 48
1. Martha and Janis
2. They do their homework together and eat popcorn.
3. The girls go to the park.
4. Martha uses her skates, and Janis uses her scooter. Sometimes they go on the swings and slides.
5. Answers will vary.

Answer Key *(cont.)*

Page 50
1. ten
2. a piece of cake
3. three
4. the queen ant
5. a bowl of food

Page 51
1. Taylor
2. Lindsey
3. Sharon
4. Mary
5. Danny

Page 52
1. dog + house = doghouse
2. sea + shell = seashell
3. rain + bow = rainbow
4. foot + ball = football

Page 53
 cone: party hat

cube: present

rectangular prism: tissue box

sphere: globe

cylinder: soup can

triangular prism: tent

Page 54
was, little, like, would, very, make, She, said, could, them, have, will, My, she, When, going

Page 55
First, third, and fourth T-shirts
Second and fourth T-shirts
Second, third, and fourth T-shirts
Make sure the correct shape is used.

Page 56
1. clown
2. a cat
3. pizza
4. circle

Page 57
Answers will vary.

Page 58
1. tree
2. kitten
3. apple pie
4. skateboard
5. bed
6. shoes
7. fire
8. sky

Page 60
Answers will vary. Possible answers:

ten, cent, tear, trap, tree, pea, car, tar, part, rent, net, pet, rant, ant, carpet, ran, rat, pan, tan, ear, eat, partner, pant, peer, cart, can, tap, parent, care, pear, tape, cape, teen, creep, preen, enter

Page 61
Make sure the tally marks are correct.

Item	1	2	3	4	5	6	7	8
🌱	▓							
🐌	▓	▓						
🐟	▓	▓	▓	▓	▓			
🐠	▓	▓	▓	▓	▓	▓	▓	

Page 62
1. The children are having a parade.
2. The man in the band plays the horn.
3. I hope Grandma can see me.
4. A new day begins at sunrise.
5. Everyone smiles for the picture.

Page 63
Make sure the graph is colored correctly.

Page 64
1. cup
2. wiggle
3. riddle
4. chap
5. silk
6. rag
7. ticket
8. cake
9. low
10. brown

Page 65
1. 7 pennies
2. 1 goldfish
3. 20 marbles
4. 4 teeth
5. 3 minutes
6. 1 hour

Answer Key *(cont.)*

Page 66

Answers will vary.

Page 67

1. reading
2. 6
3. science and P.E.
4. math
5. 2 more

Page 68

1. boxes
2. dogs
3. brushes
4. benches
5. pencils
6. buzzes
7. buses
8. glasses
9. foxes
10. girls

Page 69

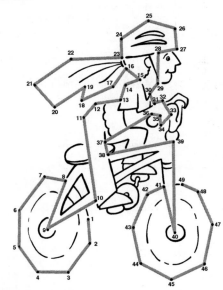

Page 70

Answers will vary.

Page 71

1. 8 peach slices
2. 1 carrot stick

Page 72

1. looking
2. opened
3. lived
4. studied
5. playing
6. cooking

Page 73

Sam lives in house number **652**.
Ana lives in house number **976**.
David lives in house number **743**.
Mei lives in house number **437**.

Page 74

2. ? question
3. ! exclamation
4. ! exclamation
5. . command
6. ? question
7. ? question
8. . statement
9. . command

Page 75

2. the number of stamps in each book
3. the number of animals Sara adopted
4. the number of rows where Larry planted his flowers

Page 76

1. Cacti grow in places where it does not rain much.
2. Their roots get as much water as they can.
3. There are more than 2,000 kinds of cacti.
4. Some are tall and thin, while others are short and round.
5. They have spines.

Page 77

2. $7 + 8 + 1 = 16$
3. $6 + 5 + 9 = 20$
4. $3 + 5 + 6 = 14$
6. $15 - 3 = 12 - 8 = 4$

Page 78

Answers will vary.

Page 79

Start → $5 - 2 = 3 + 1 =$
4
$4 + 3 = 3 - 6 = 2 +$
$=$
$7 - 1 = 6 - 2 = 4 +$
1
$10 = 1 + 9 = 4 + 5 =$
$-$
$2 = 8 - 3 = 5$ **Finish!**

Answer Key *(cont.)*

Page 80

Page 81

1. $1 + 3 + 5 = 9$
2. $8 + 10 + 1 = 19$
3. $7 + 6 + 5 = 18$
4. $3 + 2 + 5 = 10$

Page 82

Adjectives circled: neighbor's, great, tiny, taller, miniature, white, mean, bossy, loud, grouchy, back, hard of hearing, one, five

1. miniature poodle
2. white
3. tiny; no taller than the child's shin
4. very mean, bossy, and loud
5. The owner is hard of hearing and can't hear Cuddles and her barking.
6. grouchy
7. back door

Page 83

1. 6:30; little hand between the 6 and 7, big hand on the 6
2. 2:30; little hand between the 2 and 3, big hand on the 6
3. 4:30; little hand between the 4 and 5, big hand on the 6
4. 9:30; little hand between the 9 and 10, big hand on the 6

Page 84

1. shark
2. corn
3. horse
4. turkey
5. purse
6. star

ar: shark, star
or: corn, horse
ur: turkey, purse

Page 85

1. 7
2. 32
3. 18
4. 12
5. 10
6. 31

Page 86

Answers will vary.

Page 87

1. 30
2. 22
3. 55
4. 20

Page 88

1. Andy will play very well during the game.
2. Carl will learn how to swim.

Page 89

```
B P F M S K   C S I Q P L
E M I H P U A O M U E I
P W I A O A T C E D I L S
S J I L N P C K K D L T
N N U U C T H R O W D I E
T E R M H F G G S Z D N
N E T G P P U C X K I L Z
U W U I L C O C F K R U V
V A A A L U K P A O B T E
L Y Y Y E A T T S G O J Y
E R G B E P U R Z Z J N T E
K O O L V R E A D W C E
```

Page 90